Sent For One

Wendy Shelley

WestBow Press®
A Division of Thomas Nelson & Zondervan

WestBow Press books may be ordered through booksellers or by contacting:

WestBow Press
A Division of Thomas Nelson & Zondervan
1663 Liberty Drive
Bloomington, IN 47403
www.westbowpress.com
1 (866) 928-1240

ISBN: 978-1-9736-5485-8 (sc)
ISBN: 978-1-9736-5484-1 (hc)
ISBN: 978-1-9736-5486-5 (e)

Library of Congress Control Number: 2019902864

Print information available on the last page.

WestBow Press rev. date: 04/29/2019

To the Ones I Love

My husband of over four decades, David; our five children, Tennille, April, Gabriel, Vanessa, and Josiah; my children's spouses, Graham, Matthew, Bethany, Joshua, and Sarah; and our children's children, Veronica (Justin), Luke, Elijah, Sophia, Rose, Zachary, Jude, Silas, Malakhi, Anna, Thea, Charlotte, and those yet to be born—you are my treasures in earthen vessels, and I bless you all.

Contents

Introduction

Why Write Sue's Story?

Several years ago, my husband suggested to me, "Wendy, you need to write a book about Sue and share the details of your unusual friendship. It's just too fascinating a story to keep to yourself."

As I thought about his suggestion, I was hesitant initially. The Bible clearly states, "Do not let your left hand know what your right hand is doing." In other words, don't brag about your good deeds. The Catholic nun, Mother Teresa, the Saint of Calcutta, explained love and compassion best when she said, "I was just a pencil in the hand of God." And that's what I was during this journey with Sue: just a pencil.

Throughout my life, I've observed that God calls some people to serve Him in foreign, strange places. He nudges others to serve in Him in the marketplace, while some He calls to work at a coffee shop, and others still, He calls to own that coffee shop. God asks a few to proclaim His name to millions, and some, He nudges to preach in small country pulpits. But always, God reaches people one person at a time—and generally, through just *one* person.

Sue's story began in the spring of 1998 when I was in my early forties and chronicles my journey with her, which spanned over the next seventeen years.

Chapter 1

Don't Mess with Her

This is the true story of how much God loves one person. Not someone good—but rather, an alcoholic, crackhead, foul-mouthed sinner, a lady who was lost and didn't know how to be found. God sent me to her in the most unusual way. This is our story.

Raw Reality

Sitting in my car outside her shabby apartment building, I dropped my head in my hands and sobbed. You know the kind of cry—deep, heavy, heart-hurting sobs. On this cold and rainy October day, as tears trickled down my face, I cried, *Why do women do this?* I felt sick to my stomach, nauseous at the thought of it all.

I called ahead before I drove to her apartment and told her I would be there around two o'clock. I was fully aware how she wasted her money on booze, drugs, and other addictions, so I knew she would need food. Nevertheless, between when I called and arrived, someone else appeared.

Carrying grocery bags in both arms, I made my way up the dark stairs to her second-floor apartment. Shifting a few bags to free one hand, I knocked on the dilapidated door. I expected to hear her footsteps as she came to the door, but the sounds inside startled me. *What's going on?* I wondered. *Is someone else in there too?*

Fear washed over me like a cold wave. In this kind of apartment building, surprises are not welcome and are rarely positive. I stopped knocking. *I need to get out of here. Now!* I thought. *I'll just leave the groceries outside the door.* I faced the stairwell, ready to run down as fast as I could, when I heard her snarl from inside the apartment, "Who is it?" I could tell by her nasty tone she had completely forgotten I was coming.

With trepidation, I replied, "It's Wendy."

I heard her mumble incoherently, then bark, "Come back in ten."

I made my way back down the squeaky stairs. With each step, the groceries seemed heavier, but indeed, it was my heart that was now weighed down with concern and anguish. I trudged back to my car and set the food on the passenger seat. After closing the door, I collapsed in a heap and wept. I tried to pull myself together but couldn't. "Oh, Lord Jesus, Your heart must break as mine is breaking now."

I was told to come back in ten minutes, but just to be safe, I decided to make it twenty. Once again, I gathered the groceries and walked softly up the stairs. As I neared the top, I heard her door close. I glanced up just in time to see a man leave the apartment. *Oh no, not him,* I thought. I knew this man. He has a wife and kids, and I collected rent from their apartment too. When he saw me, he lowered his head and kept walking toward the rear entrance, where the stairs hugged the back of the building. I shook my head in disbelief.

Collecting Rent

I was married young and had my first child in my early twenties. I was a stay-at-home mom for twenty-five years. With five kids in my family, I was always busy and on the move. My husband worked in property management, and this building was in his portfolio. For a short while, he needed extra help with collecting the rent. Before online banking, the renters paid with cash, which meant someone had to go and collect the money in person.

"Would you help for a few months?" my husband asked. "Could you collect the rent and bring the money to the office?"

"Sure. I can do that," I said.

At the start of each month, I went to each building, knocked on every door, announced who I was, and collected the money. It usually took a few days to catch everyone home, especially in her building. Sometimes the tenants wouldn't quite have enough, and I would have to come back the next day. Surprisingly, I began to like the job.

Whenever I went to her door, she always had the correct amount. *At least I don't have to keep coming back here,* I thought. Every month was the same. I knocked and said who I was, and because the apartment doors were thin, I could hear her footsteps quite easily as she shuffled around her apartment. I would hear the click of the security chain and see the door begin to open, but it always stopped with barely a one-inch gap as she stuffed a wad of cash with her smoke-stained fingers through the opening in the door. Month after month, I never saw this lady's face—her shuffled steps, her fingers, and her cash were all I knew her by.

"Thank you," I said kindly after taking the money from her scrawny fingers. She shut the door.

After a couple months of this bizarre exchange, I asked her neighbor, "Do you know anything about the lady in apartment number six?"

The neighbor scoffed, "Oh, she's a drunk. She drinks from morning 'til night. Don't mess with her. She's nasty and mean."

A little surprised and taken aback, I replied, "Oh, okay."

Note to self. Don't mess with her. Leave her alone. I'm glad I asked.

I Finally See Her

Every month, I went to her door, the door to apartment number six, and received the same response. She unlatched the door, found her money, handed it out through the crack, and swiftly shut the door. *She doesn't want to be bothered,* I thought, *and that's okay. I won't bother her.*

Around month seven or eight, I knocked on her door and expected the same routine to play out.

"Hi, it's Wendy. I'm here to collect your rent."

I waited and heard the security chain unlatch, and then the door opened. This time, however, it didn't stop at the usual one-inch gap. This time, the door swung fully open to reveal the lady from apartment number six. I saw her for the first time; my eyes locked on hers.

"Hi," she said, "my name is Sue."

"Oh, hello, Sue," I said kindly, not wanting to say too much—inherently afraid she would slam the door.

She stood in front of me, a waif of a human being. She was thin—merely skin covering bones. Scraggily, matted, bleached-blond hair faintly touched her shoulders. Her frame was small, but she looked tough—a curious mix of hardness and fragility. She had a cigarette hanging out of one side of her mouth, and as she puffed, her eyes squinted. There was no question life had been cruel. She looked mean, just as her neighbor said.

While the smell of smoke drifted my way, I thanked her for the rent. Behind her small frame, her apartment looked disheveled. Before I could say another word, she acted quickly to end the exchange.

"You're welcome," she blurted, and with that, she shut the door. Just like that, the door she opened wide, slammed shut, with the sound of the security chain latching back on to its precarious place on the inside of the door.

With the door to apartment number six slammed in my face, I stood there, her neighbor's words ringing cautiously in my ear—"don't mess with her"—and I understood why.

Unexpected Welcome

The next month when I knocked on Sue's door for our regular routine and announced who I was, she immediately opened the door. *Wow, that's surprising,* I thought. This time, Sue left the door open and ran back inside. "Don't mess with her," the neighbor's cautionary tale, was playing in my mind as I waited anxiously. I knew I could run down the stairs, if needed.

I tried not to look around inside the mysterious apartment number six, but I couldn't resist. My eyes were pulled in to the black hole the lady—Sue—seemed to live in. The wallpaper was peeling off; the walls were stained yellow from years of smoke. The place smelled terrible too. There was stuff everywhere—garbage on the floor and empty containers on every surface. The apartment was a mess.

Sue reappeared from a corner room. "Here you go, Wendy," she said with a smile.

I was relieved. "Thank you, Sue," I said warmly.

"You're welcome," she said, and closed the door.

A month later, I knocked and again, she opened the door quickly. "Would you come in, Wendy?" she asked.

Without hesitation, I replied, "Yes, I will." It was a nudge from God.

I stepped into her apartment and closed the door behind me. *What a dirty place,* I thought. The apartment was small. I could see all the rooms from the main area where I stood. In the living room in front of me, there was one cloth chair in the corner. Years of smoke and dirt had left the well-worn material an indiscriminate shade of brownish-gray. A single, rickety wooden chair sat next to an equally rundown card table. Along the wall, there was a lumpy futon, folded down into a bed with a tattered blanket crumpled up on one end.

"Sit down," she said.

I quickly surveyed my options and decided to sit on the wooden chair, the only piece of furniture without fabric, without taking off my coat or shoes.

The kitchen was clearly visible to the left from where I was sitting. It was a mess. The dishes were piled high in the sink, still splattered with leftover food. I noticed an open bag of bread on the counter and garbage piled so high that it had spilled over onto a dirty, almost sticky floor. Looking to my right, I saw her bedroom. A crumpled piece of fabric that was once a sheet was strewn across an old mattress. A worn-out blanket lay balled up next to the stained sheet. Clothes had been tossed on the floor, and everywhere you looked, in every room, there were empty beer and liquor bottles.

I sat in quiet shock. I'd never been in a place like this, nor with a person like this in my life. *This is simply unbelievable,* I thought.

She seemed kind of quiet, somewhat subdued—and rightly so. She didn't know me. We talked for several minutes. She wondered where I lived, and I told her. I asked how long she had lived in this apartment, and she said a couple of years. After a few more minutes of idle talk, she gave me her rent money. As always, she had the full amount.

"You'll come next month?"

"Yes, I will, Sue." And with that, I left.

Little did I know then, I would continue to visit her for the next seventeen years and that one day, she would call me her best friend.

Far-Apart Lives

My life could not have been more opposite from Sue's. I was raised by good, loving parents and had two sisters, Brenda and Lynda. Our dad and mom taught us about God and modeled a life devoted to Him. I lived on a farm in the country, had five children, and was married for many years. On any given day, there was a lot to juggle in my home—bus routines in the morning and part-time jobs for my teenagers at night. There was supper to make and kids to drive here and there. There were eggs to gather and horses to feed. Put simply, I wasn't looking for something else to do. I did not need someone to have tea and chat with. My life was full to the brim, in a good way. God had an interruption planned for me though, an unexpected assignment to fulfill.

Why Is She on My Mind?

There were many tenants like Sue, and the buildings my husband managed were full of them. Sue lived in an apartment over a barber shop with her stairwell door to the left of the barber's entrance. That stairwell led to four different apartments. A few days after my first living room encounter with Sue, I started thinking about her again. *Unusual,* I thought. *Why would Sue cross my mind?*

Slowly but surely, a new pattern began to emerge. Every month when I went to collect the rent from Sue's building, she invited me in. Sue was an addict. We had nothing in common. I didn't drink with her. I didn't smoke. I didn't use drugs. She apologized every time she swore. I felt like a fish out of water. She appeared to like me, but why?

Wendy, just collect the rents and go home, I thought. *Just do your job. You're here to fill a vacant position, help for a short while, and be done. You're not here to make friends. You know nothing about her. You'll get yourself in trouble. Don't get involved. Smarten up,* I scolded myself.

Try as I might, though, I couldn't erase the mental picture of this scared little lamb trying to survive in a cruel, harsh world. I was drawn to this tiny lady who lived in apartment number six and had no idea why. I had no idea, in fact, that it was God who was sending me.

Beds and Blankets

Sue chain smoked. Sitting in her living room, she would light one cigarette after another. If smoke drifted my way, I learned to turn my head. If I wasn't quick enough, it went straight in my eyes, burning. One afternoon, when my head was turned to avoid a plume of smoke, I noticed the worn blanket on her bed. *That cover is so thin. How can she ever stay warm?* I thought.

I looked across at Sue and blurted, "Your blanket looks so worn. Can I bring you a new one?"

With a cigarette balanced between her yellowing fingers, she stopped and stared at me. She didn't say a word, and I thought, *Oh no. I must have offended her!*

After a moment, though, she replied, "Yes."

"Okay, Sue," I said, "next time I'm in town, I'll bring you a blanket."

A week later, I called to say I'd drop by. I parked in front of her building, which was screaming for a coat of paint, and made my way up the narrow, creaky stairs. The whole stairwell smelled of cigarette smoke that day. It seemed every apartment was leaking the noxious fumes. I didn't take a deep breath, saving my lungs from the scratchy burn that would ensue if I inhaled the smoke.

Standing on the top landing, I knocked on her door. She opened the door to apartment number six quickly, and I presented her with a brand-new blanket. She stood in front of me and didn't move.

"It's for you," I said. "Please take it." I handed it to her.

She reached for the blanket and brought it to her face.

"It's so soft!" she gasped. "I've never had a blanket like this." As she stroked it like fur on a kitten, she whispered, "Thank you."

"You're welcome, Sue, I'm glad you like it. It will keep you warm."

"I love it," she said excitedly in her gruff smoker's voice.

She brought the blanket to her face again, soaking in its softness. For a moment, a brief flash of time, she was lost in a stranger's kindness and generosity. She wanted to put the blanket on her bed right away. As we spread it out on the threadbare sheet, I noticed her pillow was flat as a pancake. Everything was worn out. Even the pillowcase was tattered.

"Sue, it looks like you need a little more than a blanket," I said. "How about I buy you some sheets and a pillow, and I'll talk to my husband about getting you a mattress."

She didn't know what to say. Her silence was paired with a blank, confused stare.

"Would you like that? Can I do that for you?"

"Yes," was all that came out of her mouth, but I knew what she was thinking: Would I really bring her all those things? A mattress, pillow, and sheets? *Why would the stranger who knocks at my door each month to collect rent bring me these things?*

She looked both hopeful and disappointed at the same time. She'd been let down before, too many times to count. Why would I be any different?

From what I could gather from my monthly visits, Sue lived alone. She was unloved and uncared for. My heart ached for her. Without thinking, I took a step forward and reached my arms around her. In that moment, it didn't matter that she was dirty and smelled like smoke, nor did it matter that she was a stranger. It seemed right at that moment, so I hugged her. She felt like a child in my arms, desperate to feel love. She lingered in the embrace, and so did I.

Something was happening. I could feel it. *Does God want me to be a friend to Sue? To help her? God must be sending me,* I concluded. There was no other reason I'd be standing in this dingy apartment hugging a drug addict. This was purposeful. It was intentional. I was being sent-for-one.

Chapter 2

Love Never Fails

Yes, a Mattress!

I mentioned Sue's plight to my husband, David; he quickly agreed that we needed to help her. That same week, we were chatting with a friend, and during the conversation, it just so happened that he mentioned he had just purchased a new mattress.

I interjected daringly, "What did you do with your old one?"

He told us he had his old one in storage and wondered why we asked. When we explained our reason, he was more than happy to give us the mattress. *What perfect timing!* I thought. God supplied exactly what we needed, when we needed it.

I called Sue and told her we were coming.

"You are? With a real mattress to sleep on?" she asked with skepticism.

"Yes, Sue, a real mattress!" I said decisively.

Later that week, we loaded the mattress onto our truck and drove the ten minutes into town. Parking adjacent to the outside door of the building, we unloaded the mattress and inched our way up the two flights of stairs. It was a tricky climb, heaving and hoeing up each creaky step, but we made it to the upper landing without incident.

Hearing the commotion in the stairwell, we got up the stairs and noticed Sue's door was wide open. She was waiting in the doorway. Before bringing the mattress into her apartment, I introduced her to David. Her interaction with men had always given her a reason to be frightened, and I didn't want her to be skeptical of him. The day before I had assured her that she didn't need to be afraid. He was a good man. They exchanged warm hellos, and we kept moving.

She watched us curiously. Who were we anyway? Why did we come, and why did we care? She didn't know what to make of us.

Before setting up the new mattress, we removed the old one and left it standing on its end in the hallway. Then, Sue and I went to work on making up her new bed. I took the new sheets out of their pristine plastic packaging; Sue was in awe at the color. I bought purple, her favorite, and she loved them. After shaking the sheets to unsettle some wrinkles, we fit the bottom sheet perfectly onto the mattress. She stuffed her new pillows into the matching pillowcases while I placed the top sheet over the bottom fitted one. And with the blanket I had given her the week before, we covered everything. Our efforts came together beautifully, and Sue's bed looked fit for a princess. She was so happy that she was giddy—like a little girl on Christmas morning. She gratefully accepted our kindness, and even if we never showed up again, she felt as though she had won, for once. Tonight, she would sleep on a decent mattress. Tonight, she'd feel comfortable and warm.

On the way home, we stopped by the town dump and threw her mattress in the dumpster. Out with the old, and in with the new.

What's That Ya Smokin'?

After visiting Sue for several months, she became more relaxed when I was around and slowly started to trust me. If a girlfriend dropped by when I was visiting, she loved to introduce me and called me her friend.

Early on I noticed Sue's fridge was never full. I know she wasted her money, but I just couldn't see her going hungry. That's when I decided, instead of bringing food to the foodbank, I would bring it to her. Once during one of my monthly stops, I made my way up the poorly lit stairwell with my arms full of groceries and somehow knocked on her door with a free hand. She opened quickly. "Come in!" I immediately heard voices and hesitated. *She must have company,* I thought.

Sue moved a little to the left, giving me a moment to scan the living room. *A couple lady friends,* I thought. *Okay, safe enough. I'll come in, but I won't stay long.*

Laden with bags, I walked through the living room to the kitchen, which was at the back of the apartment. In this tiny square space, there was a fridge, a stove, and a sink fixed in the middle of a small counter. *I wish there was a table to put her grocery bags on,* I thought. I couldn't leave the bags on the stovetop. What if the burners were left on accidently? Sue's sink was full of dirty dishes, spilling over onto the short counter—so my only option was the floor. *How disgusting. Nasty,* I thought. I nestled the bags by the fridge in a safe pile, hoping nothing would spoil—or worse, that a mouse would be lurking, sniffing for a snack.

I walked back into the living room and parked myself on the rickety wooden chair close to the door. To be honest, all that was running through my mind was, *When can I leave?* I didn't take off my shoes or coat, which was my unspoken rule. Since I was way out of my comfort zone when visiting this building, at the very least, I was prepared to run from any apartment.

The three ladies were sitting on the futon. Sue sat beside them on the cloth chair, and I was sitting across from these four by the door. I don't mind one friend, even two is a stretch, but three—that's too many, and the next few moments proved my inclination to be right.

I'll listen to their chatter for a couple more minutes, and then I'll leave, I said to myself. *There are too many people here. When Sue opened the door and I saw she had company, I should have just given her the groceries and left.*

At this point, I was watching this small group of ladies when suddenly, they pulled out their smokes and started lighting up. Right away, I smelled something odd. I was thinking, *This doesn't smell like cigarettes*. As I watched smoke teem from their nostrils and drift out their mouths, I had an outrageous thought: *They wouldn't be smoking marijuana, would they? No, no, it can't be. But cigarettes don't smell like this …* I was debating back and forth to myself.

While I assessed my predicament, my mind was wildly racing. I glanced over at Sue's friend, and as I was watching her, she bent down to retrieve something out of her bag. She then reached to the card table for what looked like a twelve-inch square cutting board. *What is she doing?* I asked myself. On her knees, she balanced this board and grabbed a small bag containing green leaves and started rolling. *She's done this before; I can see that!* I thought.

A clearer picture emerged: Sue and her friends were smoking marijuana, and she was making more. *What have I gotten myself into now—and how do I get out?* I cried to myself.

Puffs of smoke hung in the air; my chest tightened from sheer panic. I prayed, *Oh, Jesus, I'm in trouble—terrible trouble. Please help me! I must get out of here.*

I sprung to my feet and said I needed to go; I put my hand on the doorknob and went down the two flights of stairs so fast, if I could have taken one giant leap from the top landing, I would have! I flew outside into the fresh air and took a deep breath, so deep I could feel my lungs expand. *I haven't a clue if breathing in smoke makes you high. Or must you smoke to be high? Don't be silly,* I told myself, *you can't be high by just breathing in smoke. You must smoke to be high. Oh. I just don't know …* My thinking was so jumbled. I just wanted to go home. I searched for my keys in my coat pocket and opened the car door, shaking my head in disbelief. *What just happened?*

I said to myself, *This relationship with Sue and her friends is now at the level of ridiculousness. I'm the lady who collects rent and nothing more. What on earth am I doing in an apartment watching ladies get high? I can't keep doing this. I'll get myself in real trouble if I don't stop.*

I drove through town—a farm wife living a farm life—and made my way to my house in the country. I didn't tell a soul where I was that afternoon. Honestly, if I had retold this episode, no one would have believed me anyway.

God's Undeniable Plan

Jeremiah 29:11 assures us that God has a plan for each of us. A plan to prosper, a plan that does no harm to us. A plan to give us hope and a future. There was no question Sue yearned for hope and a future in heaven, but she didn't know how to find either. And to understand God's love, I had to love her first.

In the early years of knowing her, I often thought of a missionary story I heard in my twenties. Unquestionably, this servant became the hands and feet of Jesus on earth. Let me explain.

A missionary who felt his calling was evangelism made his way from village to village. He longed to explain to anyone who would listen what the death and resurrection of Jesus meant and that by knowing Jesus personally, you could have eternal life. However, not long into his journey, he encountered a sinister enemy bearing the name of starvation. In every village, he noticed the ground was parched, confirming no rain had touched this corner of the earth in a very long time. The people were hungry and thirsty, donning bloated stomachs and hollow eyes, a visible sign of drought and famine.

How can I tell them about a Savior when they are starving? he thought to himself.

He saw the calling within the calling, and the next week, he returned with food and water. The villagers began to watch for him, and week after week, they eagerly awaited his arrival. At long last, someone had come to help them.

Unbeknown to him, another missionary came through the village and did share the good news; he told them about a man named Jesus who could save them.

The villagers listened intently and suddenly started laughing. "Oh, we understand what you're saying now," they said in one accord. "We know this Jesus you are talking about."

The missionary was flabbergasted. "You do?" he asked. He had been under the impression they were unreached with the gospel of Jesus Christ.

They spoke on. "He comes every week and brings us food and water. Yes, we know this Jesus you are talking about. He does bring us hope, and just like you said, he has saved us."

I often reflect on this narrative. Sometimes in our effort to speak the gospel, we neglect to show the gospel. Oftentimes, by meeting a practical need, the door will also open to meet a spiritual need. After months of hard work, the missionary earned an audience with the villagers and followed up on the good news the itinerant missionary had shared. He told them about Jesus, the Savior. Jesus, who forgives sins and changes lives.

I love this missionary story. By displaying the hands and feet of Jesus so practically, many villagers came to know the Savior, the Lord Jesus Christ, and their lives were changed for all of eternity. It's a visual I'll never forget.

"Why, Wendy?"

A year or two into my journey with Sue, as we chatted about nothing really, maybe the weather, her eyes looked troubled one day, and I wondered why. Her brow was wrinkled, and before I even knew the question she was about to pose, she was searching my face for an answer.

"Is something wrong, Sue? What's the matter?" I asked in a gentle manner. Since Sue had experienced so much harshness in her life, I kept the delivery of my words very kind.

She lowered her face, looking so much older than her thirty-eight years. "Why are you helping me, Wendy? Why do you care? Why are you here? I've never met anyone like you. Please tell me the truth." She had never questioned my motives before.

"Sue," I replied, "it's because God loves you, and He sent me to tell you."

"God?" she asked. Sue went on to say, "Oh, Wendy, I've done some very bad things to ever be loved by God."

I moved closer, put my arm around her love-deprived body, and said, "He doesn't care about that. He loves you and sent me to tell you."

The word *love* meant nothing to Sue. How do you understand love when your definition of love is so skewed? The notion of me loving her without anything in return didn't make sense; to her, love always had a price tag.

Life has taught me, unmistakably, that every person on this planet just wants to be loved. Right from infancy until the hour we draw our last breath, something deep within our souls yearns to be loved, wanted, and accepted. It's a worldwide longing and a universal ache: please—somebody, anybody—tell me I belong and that you care whether I live or die.

God sent me to fulfill Jeremiah 29:11 in Sue's life. He had a plan for her, and in His plan, God included me. That brings me to a wonderful conclusion: God always has a plan and, it's a perfect one, with eternity in mind.

Hospitals

Sue's health was not good when I met her at thirty-seven, let alone as each birthday passed. Between alcohol, drugs, cigarettes, and sin of all sorts, Sue was slowly destroying her physical body. Her voice was gruff and raspy, her lips had a smoker's wrinkle, and her face was aged beyond her years.

She was often sick from one germ or another, and even a cold kept her down for weeks. If I called and she didn't pick up for days, I would phone the hospital, and sure enough, she had been admitted. I decided to give her my phone number and told her to call me if she had an emergency. Even in those early years, I wondered how long she would live.

Once I drove to the hospital and stopping on the correct floor, asked at the nurses' station for her room number. The nurse grabbed her chart, flipped a few papers over, and asked for my name. I said who I was, and with her head down, she replied, "Oh, I see you are her next of kin."

A stunned looked came across my face. Powerless to conceal my shock, I said weakly, "I am?"

The nurse, with her eyes peering over her glasses, looked up and slowly replied, "You don't know if you are the next of kin?"

I felt as though I was caught in a lie, only I wasn't lying. I thought, *Next of kin? Who writes down a name of someone you casually know as your next of kin?* I couldn't conceive of such a thing.

I quickly changed my tone and firmly said, "Yes I am." The nurse knew something was up and reluctantly gave me her room number. To be honest, I couldn't blame the nurse. How could you not know if you were the next of kin to someone who was lying in a hospital bed that you came to visit?

I trudged toward Sue's room with a heavy heart of sadness. Sue only had me? For just this short period of time we had known each other, she wrote my name down as the closest person she has on earth? That was the saddest thing I had heard in a long time.

Sue hated the hospital, mostly because she couldn't drink, smoke, or pop pills there. More than once, when the nurses weren't looking, she would get dressed and sneak out a side door without telling anyone.

"Sue, the hospital staff are trying to help you. You can't just walk out. You must be signed out by the doctor!" I would tell her.

"They don't care about me," she said adamantly.

"Yes, they do, Sue. They're trying to make you better."

"No, they're not!" she barked angrily.

There was no use arguing with her. If truth be told, to look after her as a patient would have required a lot of patience!

One day, she told me, "I fired my doctor."

"You fired your doctor? You can't fire a doctor! Sue, doctors are there to keep you alive. Without them, you won't live. You can't be walking out on doctors. They don't like that." She looked up at me with the eyes of a child who had just been told the truth by their mother—and she didn't say another word.

Addictions

Adding to Sue's list of addictions—drugs, alcohol, and tobacco—was prescription drugs. Like many addicts, she didn't hesitate to sell her pain medication for cash.

"I get good money for these on the street," she would tell me.

"Oh, Sue, you shouldn't be doing that. The pills were prescribed for you in good faith by your doctor!" She knew it was wrong to sell the pills, but unwise people do unwise things.

Another time, I visited her and noticed she wasn't smoking.

"Sue, you're not smoking anymore?" I knew this observation couldn't be true, but I asked the question anyway.

"I've slowed down. I buy smokes cheap and sell them to my friends for more."

Just when I thought I'd heard it all, Sue told me something new.

As soon as she recovered from a stint of sickness, she would hit the bottle again. I didn't like talking to her or visiting her when she was drinking. If I called and her speech was noticeably slurred, I assumed she was drunk and postponed my visit. However, sometimes her drunkenness caught me by surprise. On one such occasion, she opened the door and it was obvious: she was plastered. Peering around her body, I observed empty beer and liquor bottles, everywhere: empties on the card table, the small side table, and the floor, causing the smell of liquor to infuse the air.

"Sue," I said tenderly as I remained at the door, "this is no way to live. Drinking won't help you, and drugs won't fix your problems. God loves you, Sue. He cares for you. He sent me to tell you."

She reached out her arms for me to hold her, and with her head on my shoulder, she whispered, "I love you, Wendy," and she meant it.

Truthfully, she had no idea how to live any other way.

God's Love

In all the years of knowing Sue, I had never muttered the words, "I'll never go back." I certainly didn't agree with her lifestyle choices; however, echoing the missionary, God's love in action was what she needed to see. I've since learned that when God calls you to something, He equips you as well. As Mother Teresa says, "I am just a pencil in the hand of God"—and that's what I was, just a pencil.

Sue would look at me with big, longing eyes and like droplets of water on a thirsty rose, absorb the words, "I love you" every time I said them.

As strange as this relationship was—and clearly, it was out of the ordinary—I kept coming back to Sue like a magnet. Did she take advantage of my kindness over the years? Absolutely. Did she use me? Most certainly. Sometimes, though, love is messy.

My sent-for-one assignment was to a drug addict, an alcoholic, and someone who had a lifestyle I knew nothing about. But it proved this scripture to be true:

Love is patient, love is kind. It does not envy, it does not boast, it is not proud. It does not dishonour others, it is not self-seeking, it is not easily angered, it keeps no record of wrongs. Love does not delight in evil but rejoices with the truth. It always protects, always trust, always hopes, always perseveres. Love never fails. (1 Corinthians 13:4–8 NIV)

CHAPTER 3

On the Flipside

"Tilly's Dead"

"What do you mean, Tilly's dead?" I exclaimed. I knew Tilly had been ill for several weeks, but I never expected an imminent death.

"She's gone, Wendy. She died last night," Sue said sorrowfully.

Tilly was one of Sue's apartment friends, whom she had known for a long time. The tenants who lived in Sue's building were a tight group, as most of them had little or no family, and if they did have anyone, they seldom came to visit. Tilly was the older of the bunch, a lonely widow, and her apartment friends looked out for her. When I went to her door to collect her rent, she often invited me in for tea. I was usually on the run; however, if my heart strings pulled that day, I could rarely say no.

Sue continued, "Wendy, this morning the phone rings and the display says 'Tilly' calling. I was scared to death. I didn't want to answer!" Her voice began escalating until she had worked herself into a frenzy. "I got so spooked and thought Tilly was calling me from the grave!"

"Sue, oh Sue, you know dead people don't make phone calls. There must be another explanation." Turns out, Tilly's daughter was in her mom's apartment and saw Sue's number by her mom's phone and called to see who Sue was.

"Dear Tilly. I'm going to miss her!" Sue said reflectively.

Would You Take Us, Please?

My phone rang the next morning.

"The three of us want to go to Tilly's funeral. Would you take us?"

I had never met Tilly's family. Pictures of her children and grandchildren hung on her apartment wall, surrounded by a large photo of happier days with her husband; but to my knowledge, no one ever came to see her. Taking this group to Tilly's funeral was a bit risky, mainly because her family was unknown to me, and to make matters worse, Tilly was resting in our town's oldest, most prestigious, funeral facility. My first thought after Sue asked was, *You are kidding, right? Take the three of you to a funeral?* I didn't mind my apartment friends on their turf, but taking them out to my turf—well, that's another story. As I think back now, I'm ashamed of my judgmental thoughts. I was more concerned with how I looked accompanying the three of them than how they felt wanting to give their last respects to a good friend.

I finally agreed to take them. "I'll pick the three of you up at one fifteen Thursday afternoon. Be at the front door of your building, and you tell the others." Sue assured me they would be ready, and since none of them drove, they would be waiting and on time—that I knew for sure.

Thursday Afternoon

Knowing my friends wouldn't have the proper funeral attire, my thought was to dress down myself. After surveying my closet, I opted for a middle-of-the-road choice: black pants and shirt, nothing too fancy.

As it turned out, my clothes didn't help one bit.

It was a bitter cold February day—a horrible day for a funeral. I drove down the main street in our small town and turned right onto the side street creeping closer to their building; you couldn't miss the emerald green door. I glanced over, and my eye caught a glimpse of my threesome. *What are they doing huddled together?* I said to myself. As I took a closer look, they were puffing profusely, smoking quickly.

They wore their best. Well-worn ski jackets, winter boots with the laces dangling, wool hats with tassels, heavy knitted scarfs, and large fingerless mitts all put together without any color coordination. *Oh my, this is going to be interesting!* I thought.

I stopped in front of the door and beeped. They waved, dropped their smokes onto the sidewalk, snuffed them out with the heels of their boots, and hopped in. By the time I got to the funeral home, the smoke smell had permeated my car, and I smelled like I had been smoking too. We were going to be quite a foursome.

As I made a right turn into the parking lot, I noticed the funeral director standing just inside the grandiose doors, welcoming each guest as they arrived. He looked quite distinguished in his three-piece black suit, a stark contrast to the guests he was about to greet.

Before we exited the car, they asked, "Is Tilly in this funeral home?"

"Yes," I replied as I opened their doors. "She's inside. Come with me."

Funeral Time

There was quite a lineup as we shivered in the cold. I hoped no one would give way to idle chatter while we waited with our teeth chattering. When our turn came, with a slight grin, he opened the door for me, and my trio trailed behind. I felt a little odd. *Did he just look down on me?* I thought. *No, he couldn't have. It must be my imagination.* I had been to this funeral home dozens of times before and had never felt slighted. *My mind must be playing tricks,* I concluded.

My friends walked in behind me, and as I turned to make sure they were coming, I observed the funeral director's face. *It's not my imagination. He doesn't want us here!* Little did I realize that I was about to experience what life is like on the "flipside."

My friends were used to being slighted, and the funeral director's reaction didn't faze them one bit. I noticed, but they didn't. This trio walked right past him, not giving him the time of day. They couldn't have cared less who he was, or how he was dressed, or that he owned the place. They were there to see Tilly, and that was all that mattered. Humorously, they marched right in like they owned the place!

It was about to get worse, though. Much worse.

We walked into a crowd of well-dressed family members, all lingering around the bustling visiting area. Tilly's open casket was at the front of the room surrounded by large displays of flowers and lovely baskets of indoor plants. I surveyed the guests and identified the immediate family. One of them took a quick glance our way, and I smiled nervously. I could feel her questioning eyes land upon us and worse, her unfriendly, piercing gaze upon my friends. She had the same look as the funeral director, a stare that begs, "What are you doing here? You don't belong."

In the family's defense, and to be perfectly honest, we did look out of place. Seldom do you see folks in ski jackets with tassel hats in funeral homes; although I looked like a regular guest, I was shunned right along with my three friends.

"Wendy, who are these people?" Sue asked in her raspy talking voice. "Tilly doesn't know these people. I've never seen any of them before!" They were stunned at the number of people in the visiting room. They couldn't get over it.

"Shhh," I whispered with my finger to my lips. "Not too loud. She must have lots of friends and family." I wished they had whispered their thought. I didn't want to admit that we were making a scene. *How could this be happening?* I thought.

"Family?" Sue's friend said with surprise. "Family, she didn't have any family. What family?"

This afternoon was quickly going from bad to worse.

Snubbed and Shunned

Suddenly, I felt hot and flushed and took off my coat and laid it over my arm. "Shhh," I whispered, "we have to be quiet." They didn't pay any attention to my appeal.

Trying to fix this problem, like a mother hen with three chicks trailing behind, I walked over to a well-dressed lady in a navy-blue suit with matching high heels, who I assumed was Tilly's daughter—perhaps the same daughter who had called Sue from her mom's apartment. Courageously, I began, "These are Tilly's friends from her apartment building. They wanted to come to her funeral. They were good friends of your mother, and I've brought them because they wanted to say their final goodbyes."

Without a smile, she shot back with one word: "Oh." Immediately, I felt insulted. She didn't want any of us here. She didn't like the look of her mom's friends and included me in the group.

By now, the family was glancing my way and I hardly knew what to do. Clearly, we were not welcome. This was a place for respectable folk, not people like us. To be bluntly honest, I wanted to shout to the family, "I've just brought your mother's friends to the funeral home. Don't look at me that way. Don't toss me in the mix. I'm not one of them; I'm really one of you!"

To my disgrace, I began to say to Tilly's daughter, "I don't live in the apartment building where they live, I just collect their rent…" but she turned away. Oh, my heart. I had just been ignored and now to have someone turn their back on me—I couldn't stand it! What an afternoon this was. I was getting a taste of what it was like to live on the flipside—and it sure didn't feel good.

My trio was oblivious to the exchange that had just happened. They were more appalled at seeing her family surrounding the casket, looking remorseful, sad that their mother had passed away.

"I've never seen these people, Wendy," they said, and they didn't care who heard them. They had nothing to prove and no image to protect; they didn't pretend to be someone they weren't, and they didn't care what people thought of them. Clearly, I had a lot to learn from the trio I was so quick to disconnect myself from.

As we walked closer to the casket, I was careful not to look to the left or right. I kept my eyes fixed straight ahead. My trio was visibly emotional when they saw Tilly, and rightly so; they genuinely loved her. Even though we were shunned, I stood behind them like a lioness, protecting them while each one said their goodbyes. After a few minutes, I whispered, "We should let others see her now," and they followed me away from the casket.

The service was in the open chapel area, about twenty feet from the casket. They followed me to a row of chairs about midway back, and we sat down. I sat at the beginning of the aisle, and one by one, they all filed in. Since the previous twenty minutes had been disastrous, I wondered how this was going to go—not for them of course, but for me.

I whispered, "Shhh, the funeral is starting." They just looked at me with blank stares. This funeral had too much hypocrisy for them already. They didn't live in a fake world.

They stayed silent during all the "lies," they told me after. I breathed a sigh of relief, thankful that none of them spoke up during the funeral and corrected the "lies." Can you imagine if they had?

The funeral director rose to give further instructions. "The family has prepared a lunch for all present. It's in our fellowship hall next to this building. Everyone is welcome." With all the chaos of the funeral, I had completely forgotten about a lunch. *Oh, no,* I thought. *For sure they will want to go, and I know the family won't want to see them, or me, in any fellowship hall.* And just as I suspected, they heard "lunch" and wanted to go. Of course, free food!

"Okay," I smiled.

Some funeral lunches are not really lunches but merely snacks with an unspoken etiquette. You fill a small plate with a little food and engage in light conversation. However, knowing my hungry friends, I couldn't see that happening. *Can this day get any worse?*

We put our arms in our coats and buttoned them up; they pulled their toques over their ears, slipped their hands in their oversized mitts, and out we went. The funeral home was once an old, majestic home, and the adjacent older homes were not too far apart. To accommodate larger crowds, the funeral home purchased the house beside it, and that became the fellowship hall.

Once outside, they rummaged in their pockets, found their cigarettes, and started smoking as fast as they could. I waited in front of the stately brown doors until they had sufficient puffs, and after they squished what was left with their boots, we went inside.

The Unforgettable Funeral Lunch

Thankfully, we were one of the first groups to arrive. My trio followed me through the big parlour of this stunning old home into the fellowship area, and I must say, the food presentation was exquisite. They never ate anywhere upscale, and with such an abundance of food, their eyes were as big as saucers. The sandwiches were nicely displayed on three-tiered plates, and the vegetables were perfectly cut and presented on large platters with matching bowls of dip. There was a beautiful assortment of fruit displayed in seamless order on delicate glass serving plates, and then there was the cheese and crackers. A lovely variety, all set out orderly and presented attractively on matching plates. There was an assortment of drinks, including tea and coffee, and then the dessert table. Oh my, the desserts! A long table top arrayed in an elegant white lace tablecloth abounding with squares, cookies, and pastries of all sorts. It was a sight to behold!

I breathed deeply. "Can we eat now?" they said in unison. Not looking to the left or right, I motioned for them to come with me.

My threesome piled their plates as high as they could—sandwich on top of sandwich. Their vegetables barely stayed on their plates as the dip nipped along the sides. I stood back and watched them take whatever they wanted. By this time, I was a little annoyed at how they had been treated—at how we had been treated—and I really didn't care who was looking at us. I scanned the room for a place to sit down, and didn't look anyone in the eye.

I whispered, "Okay, let's sit over here," and motioned to a table by the window.

I looked straight ahead and took my place at the table. I had enough of trying to justify myself and appear "proper" to a family I'd never seen before. I was tired of trying to justify that I was better than the friends their mother loved. How disgraceful to even think thoughts such as that; I was ashamed of myself. We were a foursome now, and I was one of them. End of story.

After finishing their sandwich plates, my threesome walked over to the dessert table and loaded up. I didn't care if their pastries were falling off their plates or who was looking if they did; the flipside was a hard place to live and for my friends, that was their day-to-day reality. Once they gobbled all their sweets, I said, "Perhaps we should go now?" Yes, they were ready. We took our coats from the back of our chairs, bundled up for the weather outside, and left the building. Not surprisingly, no one said goodbye to us.

I dropped my friends off and did some soul searching. Why on earth was I trying to impress people I would never see again? And why did I seek validation from strangers who didn't care one iota about me? This trio had taught me a few things.

On the Outs

Surprisingly, Jesus was often on the flipside, and like my friends, He was used to it. When He lived on earth, some people liked Him, and others did not. Interestingly, He didn't care, either. Jesus had dinner with Zacchaeus, and he was a thief. He healed lepers to the disdain of the righteous folk. He ate supper with sinners and didn't care where they came from. He talked to the Samaritan woman, who was an outcast in her day. Truly, Jesus cared for those on the flipside and didn't think much of the lofty and proud.

After my funeral experience, my sent-for-one assignment seemed reversed that day. God was speaking to me, and I was the one!

Chapter 4

Her World Is Harsh

I Lost My Mind

I parked in front of Sue's apartment building and walked through the faded emerald green outside door. As soon as I turned the corner at the bottom of the square stairwell landing, I heard shouting coming from an apartment on the second floor. Since there were only two apartments on the top floor, I knew it either had to be Sue's or the single lady, Victoria, who lived across the hall.

I cautiously crept up the stairs. *I really don't want to be here now,* I thought. *Where are the voices coming from?* I took a few more steps and abruptly stopped halfway up. *I hear yelling, and I can't stand it! If it's Sue's apartment, I'm not barging in on an argument.* To be honest, fighting and arguing upsets me. In my lifetime, rarely have I allowed such behavior in myself or those in my family.

Once my foot landed on the top stair, I knew the commotion was coming from the apartment across from Sue's—and it wasn't just arguing. There were shouts and cries of distress. The lady who lived there was clearly in trouble. Instantly, I could hear the thump of my heart as fear gripped my entire body. I knocked on Sue's door in rapid succession, and she opened it quickly.

"Sue, something is dreadfully wrong in apartment number seven!"

She replied without a trace of emotion, "Oh, sounds like Victoria's getting beat up."

I stood there dumbfounded and wondered if I heard her correctly. *What did she just say?* With my brow furrowed, I replied, "What do you mean 'Victoria's getting beat up'?"

Having been so desensitized by life, Sue shrugged her shoulders and nonchalantly replied, "Oh, she meets these workers in the bars and lets them in."

We lived in a farming community, and during the summer months, our local farmers would hire workers to assist in planting and harvest. For the most part, these workers were in our area for just that: to work. However, there are a few bad apples in every barrel, and with the bars full of farmhands on weekends, sadly, there were some with bad intentions.

The scuffling continued until I heard a bloodcurdling scream. Something came over me at that moment, and I don't quite know what it was. For lack of a better explanation, I completely lost my mind. With Sue standing in her doorway, I turned, took a couple quick steps across the hall, and started pounding on apartment seven's door as hard as I could.

"Hey, what's going on in there?" I yelled as I banged my fists. "What's going on?"

A loud scream pierced the air, and a male voice began to spew out foul and angry words. I listened as furniture slid across the floor and heard chairs being tossed about. *Oh, no! She's getting hurt,* I cried internally.

I thumped louder. "Hey you, cut it out!" I kept pounding. "Stop it!" Again, my urges were followed by a bunch of cursing and the sound of stuff being thrown around while her hysterical screams continued. Frantically, I grabbed the doorknob and turned it clockwise as fast as I could. I heard a click: it was unlocked.

Instinctively, I pushed the door open with my shoulder, and the scene before me was appalling. Her apartment looked like a war zone, with everything out of place. My eyes quickly landed on a giant of a man, clutching at this poor lady. I remember him being tall and looking humongous, and because it was summertime, he wore a cut-off shirt, exposing his muscular arms. There was no question he was farm strong, and certainly no match for my frightened friend or myself.

She kept trying to stand to her feet, and even with me in the doorway, he was acting like an animal. I start screaming, "Get out! Get out of here now," and I pointed to the door. He turned his head and looked at me, cursing endlessly like an erupting volcano.

Instantly, another level of adrenalin kicked in, and I railed at him as loud as my voice would shriek, and kept pointing toward the door. "Get out, get out of here now! Leave her alone, and get out of this building!"

He glared my way with penetrating eyes and continued his obscene behavior. "Get out, I said! Leave her alone and get out! Get out of here and never come back!" and I pointed right at him again with one final "Get out!" that my frightened, yet emboldened, voice could muster.

He shoved her against the wall, and she weakly slid down, just like you see in the movies. When I think back now, I gave no thought to being attacked myself; surely God was with me.

I kept up my barrage. "Out!" *Somehow, I must make him leave,* I thought. *Jesus, please help me. I must make him go!* I backed up as far as I could with my back pressed against the open door, pushing it open as far as possible and screaming, "Get out!"

Suddenly, the beast of a man straightened his shirt and began walking toward me. I had no clue what I was going to do next. When he came within three feet of me, he looked back at the woman, pointed his surly finger, and thundered, "I'll be back for you tonight, and when I come, I'll kill you."

Reluctantly, he moved past me, and I stood as rock-solid as a statue. Toward the stairs he lumbered, and once his foot hit the top stair, I took a step into the hallway and bellowed, "You will not come back tonight! Don't you ever come in this building again. Ever!" He cursed all the way down the stairs and out the front apartment door, muddling into the street. I had never heard such foul language in my life, nor had I ever been on the receiving end of such profanity.

Picking up the Pieces

I walked back into the shattered apartment and reached for my friend. She was brokenhearted and collapsed with heavy sobs into my open arms. I said softly, "Please don't let men like him into your home. These men don't love you. They only come to hurt you. Don't talk to men like this, and never tell them where you live."

"Wendy," she said, sniffling, "he's going to come back, and when he does, he will kill me."

"No, he won't," I replied with authority. "I won't let that happen."

Words were tumbling out of my mouth before I even knew what I was saying. *How can I prevent him, this giant of a man, from coming back?* I thought. With a startling amount of courage, I assured her—and somehow, myself—again, "I will not let that happen."

After consoling her and fixing the furniture as best as I could, I slipped across the hall to Sue, who was still standing in her doorway. I didn't know what she thought of my outburst—other than she looked a bit shocked—and I wasn't about to ask.

"I couldn't stand by and do nothing, Sue. I'm sorry for the ruckus." It felt like my stomach had been turned inside out, and now, my adrenaline was taking a deep plunge. I spent a few more minutes making small talk, but I couldn't stay. "I should run along now," I said quietly. She could see I was visibly shaken, and I quickly said goodbye.

Little did I know then, but a couple years down the road, it would be Sue who was attacked, and regrettably, no one was close enough to hear her cries. Life is so cruel at times, especially for those living on the flipside.

What Now?

I left the apartment building and strained to pull myself together. For me, this traumatizing ordeal was terribly upsetting. I couldn't even imagine how my poor friend was coping after what she had just endured.

I simply have no words to describe how I felt that day. To see domestic violence up close and personal was purely horrifying. The abusive behavior I saw toward another human being, with the intent to harm them both physically and emotionally, was simply unbelievable. And this happens, everywhere, every day. My heart is so saddened.

The afternoon's altercation took up more time than I planned, and now I was running late. My children were getting off the bus, and I needed to get home.

As I drove up the laneway to my farmhouse to feed my dog, watch the bus drop off my kids, and then prepare supper and live my normal, everyday life, I said aloud in the car, "Wendy, it's time to switch gears. You must process this later. You're a mom, and your kids need your full attention. It's time to be all in." As a parent, you must give 100 percent, 100 percent of the time, every day of the week—and I reminded myself of that.

After supper and the long work week he had, my husband asked the usual, "How was your day?" He expected my standard response: "Oh you know, busy, running here and there." But instead, I made his head turn and his eyes pop when I quietly replied, "I lost my mind today."

He looked stunned and opened his mouth, spilling out, "You lost your mind? What are you talking about, you lost your mind?"

I proceeded to relive what had occurred at the apartment building that afternoon, and I confessed to him my brave declaration: I wouldn't let anything happen to her again. David listened to my story, and without a moment's hesitation, he confirmed, "You're right, we can't let that happen." Now his mind was churning to come up with a solution.

"Now, what do we do?" I asked.

"I'm not sure. Let me think about it."

Throughout the evening, he pondered his options. I'm not sure what they were; he didn't share them with me, but I knew he would come up with a plan. A little while later, he took me aside and said, "After the kids are in bed, I'll park outside the apartment building and watch the door. I won't let him go back in."

"All night?" I asked.

"If I have to, yes. What does he look like?" I gave him a description, and he assured me he wouldn't let him in.

"What will you do if he tries?" I asked.

"I don't know quite yet."

Once the kids were settled, my husband picked up the truck keys and made his way out the back door of our farmhouse. Even though he had worked all week, and certainly didn't expect to be on surveillance on his Friday night, he willingly went to help another lost soul whose path had crossed mine. I watched him walk to the barn, throw a baseball bat in the front passenger seat, and drive out the laneway. *Yikes,* I thought.

In our small town, it is easy to spot someone walking around in the middle of the night, so he parked in front of Sue's building and watched for hours. He stayed until all the bars were closed, and then another hour after that, just to be sure. Thankfully, no one approached the building.

The next morning, I phoned my friend to see how she was doing.

"He didn't come last night, Wendy."

"I know," I told her. "My husband parked in front of your building and watched the door. He wouldn't have let him hurt you again."

"Thank you, Wendy. Please thank him for me."

That giant of a man never came back to her apartment again.

The Thief of Alcohol

Excessive drinking became Sue's escape from life, and alcohol was slowly destroying her body. I smelt alcohol on her breath and on her clothes, and even the curtains in her apartment seemed to absorb the distinct smell of liquor.

No one ever decided, "Today I will become an alcoholic." When addictions spiral out of control in someone's life, the Bible gives us a clue as to who is behind these vices: "The thief comes only to steal, and kill, and destroy, but I have come that they may have life, and have it to the full" (John 10:10 NIV). The truth concerning addictions and sins of all sorts is, then, clearly spelled out in this verse: the enemy of our soul is out to kill, steal, and destroy—and I saw firsthand his destruction in Sue's life.

By this point, I had known Sue for a couple of years, and one day, I popped by with her usual monthly groceries. When she opened the door, I instantly knew something was different. *What's changed here?* I asked myself. I looked past her, and the apartment appeared tidier. Curiously, I took a slow scan of her living room, moving my eyes from side to side, and then I knew: I didn't see bottles anywhere. Not one bottle. *Very strange,* I thought. *I wonder what happened?*

After a few minutes of idle chatter, I couldn't resist asking, "Sue, it looks like you're not drinking today. That's so good. I'm very proud of you!"

"Yes," she replied as a matter of fact in her abrupt way. "No more drinkin'. The doctor told me my liver is shot and if I don't stop, I'll be dead in a year. So, I've stopped."

"You stopped?" I said shockingly. "Just like that? Cold turkey?"

"Just like that," she replied. "Cold turkey. I have to or I'll be a goner. I don't want to die."

I am unaware of what medications she took to help with such a shock to the system; however, I never saw alcohol in her apartment again. Her will to live overcame her desire to drink. Except, however, for the very few times she slipped—which were a direct result of being where she shouldn't be, with people she shouldn't be with. Otherwise, she never touched alcohol again. However, if you reflect on such a feat after drinking all your life, it is quite remarkable.

I truly loved this little lady, with no strings attached. It was such an unusual friendship, and I still struggle to describe it in words. Me, the most unlikely, was sent to love her, the most unlovely.

At this point, my sent-for-one journey wasn't even half over. Sue was in my life for many more years, with many more wild moments and concerns ahead.

Chapter 5

Sent by God

Sue's Moving, and My Job is Done

After a couple more years, Sue gave up her apartment where I collected rent, and my husband didn't need me to fill in at that job anymore. I assured Sue, though, "We are friends. I promise, I won't leave you." I don't use the word *promise* often; it's too binding of a term. However, in this case, it fit—I wouldn't leave her, and I *promised*.

Sue moved to another place, and I called to say I would drop by. It was the third week of the month, and I knew her government check wouldn't arrive for another week. She would need food. As per usual, I gave her the appointed time of my arrival: one o'clock on Tuesday. I knew she would be waiting.

I didn't like her new place. The apartment building was on the main street in our town and in worse shape than her previous one. It was in a row of double houses, and each house had a few apartments in it. The main door to her double house was a hefty, oversized, brown wooden door—which looked rather grand—and it opened into a dimly lit common area with a lone, exposed light bulb in the ceiling. *Why are these places always dimly lit with glaring lightbulbs?* I thought to myself. On either side of the foyer was an apartment. There was another apartment straight ahead, which was rented by Sue's friend, as well as one up the stairs and to the left, which was hers. The whole place gave me the creeps.

The dark, olive green steps going up to her apartment were narrow, winding, and uneven and went almost straight up. Once at the top, the door opened out but was attached to the last step so you had to back up and go down one step, and then reach up and turn the handle to open it. Puzzling and awkward to say the least. This new place and I were not friends.

It was close to one o'clock, so I gathered Sue's groceries, double-checked my car doors to make sure they were locked, and opened the door to the main foyer. Hurrying, I turned to my left and quickly made my way up the narrow stairs. I was loaded down with bags, as I didn't want to come up twice.

I knocked and waited awkwardly on the stairs, expecting Sue to answer quickly. "That's funny," I said aloud to myself. "I just called last night. Maybe the television is blaring?" However, I knew that wasn't the answer. I couldn't hear any television on in the apartment. *Maybe Sue just didn't hear me, plain and simple,* I thought. So, I knocked a little louder. My hands were now feeling the weight of the bags as I shifted my feet at the top of the stairs. I knocked again, and still, there was no answer.

Should I try the door handle? A little risky, I thought. *You just don't walk in on Sue.* By this time, though, the bags were actually too heavy to hold any longer, and the plastic handles were cutting into my fingers. I released a couple of grocery bags and supported them clumsily on my knee, hoping that the groceries wouldn't start falling out and go clunking down the stairs.

I'll try the doorknob, I finally decided. As I turned it, the door opened.

"Sue," I called out. "Sue, it's Wendy." Expecting her to finally hear me, I was instead greeted with dead silence. *This doesn't make sense. She's not home with the door open? She normally has her doors locked,* I thought.

As I walked inside, there was an eerie quietness. I put the grocery bags on the table, and kept calling her name. I opened the fridge and tried to make a racket as I put the milk and cheese on the shelf, closing the fridge door with a thud. With my foot, I pushed a chair across the floor to create a scraping noise, hoping she would hear the commotion. But all that existed was silence, and not a single sound.

Is She Dead?

This apartment is tiny. She should have heard me, I thought. The door to her bedroom was ajar, and it was right past the small, rectangular living room and to the right. With my heart beating like a drum, I inched toward her room, calling her name. *What do I do now? I can't just peek in her bedroom? Oh Jesus, help me. What do I do?* I cried.

I stood on tiptoes before the doorframe of her room, and stretched my neck forward as far as I could. I saw clothes strewn all over the place, but my eyes locked on her bed. *Is that her tiny frame lying under the covers? Why didn't she hear me when I called her name? She couldn't be in that deep of a sleep, could she?*

Cautiously, I walked into her bedroom, over to the side of the bed where she was curled up, and peered over top of her body. Unfortunately, she was curled up in the fetal position, making it impossible for me to see her chest rise and fall. *Is she alive*? I wondered. By the way she was lying in bed, I couldn't tell. Then the thought crossed my mind: *Has Sue overdosed*?

I decided to lightly tap her shoulder and see if she moved. If she didn't respond right away, I would call 911 for help.

"Sue," I whispered, "it's Wendy, Sue. I'm here."

She moved faintly. *Oh, thank goodness. Okay, I know she's alive.* I stood by her bed, wondering what to do next. After a few more minutes, I leaned down and whispered her name again. She opened one eye, just a thin crack. When she saw it was me, she garbled ever so slowly. "Wendy, it's you—I'm so sick," and with that, she laid still again. Relieved that she was still alive, I gently stroked her arm while she slept. *When she stirs again,* I thought, *I'll ask her what happened.*

Once she stirred, I bent down and quietly asked her what happened. She mumbled words, disjointedly, but I figured it out: yesterday, she fell off the wagon. *Okay,* I thought to myself, *now I understand why she's in this death-grip. She's been drinking.* I found out later that some of her friends had come by the night before and brought booze. Normally, whenever anyone brought drinks to her apartment, Sue would "kick them out," as she called it. However, that night, the pull was too strong, and because she had liver cirrhosis, Sue couldn't process the alcohol she drank. Even a small amount could make her deathly ill, which it did.

Sue was too groggy to talk and fell back to sleep. I slipped into the kitchen and locked the apartment door. I put her groceries away and went back to her room. Even though she was sleeping, I found a chair, brought it close to her bed, and spent the next hour stroking her arm and singing every chorus and hymn that came to mind. When it was time for me to leave, I kissed her forehead and made my way out the door, down the narrow, creaky stairs, picked up my teenagers from school, and went back to my real life.

That evening, my sons had hockey practice and my daughters had part-time jobs and needed a ride. And before running all over the place with the kids, everyone was hungry and needed supper. To feed our family of seven, you didn't just throw something together, nor did you pick up something. That was too expensive, I had to plan ahead—and cook. Yes, my real life didn't resemble Sue's in any way, shape, or form. Therefore, it was so unusual that God gave me such an out-of-the-box assignment.

Is This Heaven?

The next day, I called to see how Sue was doing.

"Wendy, did you come yesterday?" she asked.

"Yes, Sue, I sure did."

"Did you sing to me?" Sue asked.

"Yes, I did."

"I knew it!" she exclaimed. "When I woke up this morning, I couldn't believe I was in my bed. All through the night I heard your voice, and kept thinking, *Where am I?* This has to be heaven, because I hear Wendy singing!"

I smiled and said with a chuckle, "I'm sorry to disappoint you, Sue, but it was just me singing on earth yesterday afternoon! Your mind must have been replaying my visit throughout the night."

It is interesting to note, though, that amid Sue's dreadful reaction to alcohol, her inner person, the real Sue, was completely absorbing the divine. Through the hymns I was singing, her spirit was grasping for the life-giving words of Jesus. Truly, like the Bible says, we are fearfully and wonderfully made: body, soul, and spirit.

"Thank you for coming, Wendy. I love you."

"I love you too, my sweetheart. Don't let friends in with liquor, Sue. Just 'kick them out,' as you say. It's too tempting, and your body can't handle it. I'm glad I was there."

"I won't drink ever again. I hate falling off the wagon." And as far as I knew, she never fell off the wagon again. However, her smoking increased, as did her drug habit, as well. It's hard to fight multiple addictions.

Phone, Phones, and More Phones …

Sue never came right out and asked me but hinted that she needed a cell phone. I knew she couldn't afford one, and she didn't want to ask me to buy her one. However, now that she was moving from place to place, for my own peace of mind, I wanted—I needed—to buy her a phone.

To know someone needs help and then to make them beg is so demeaning. I wouldn't make her do that. "Sue, why don't we go to the mall, and I'll buy you a cell phone? We'll do the pay as you go plan, and I'll buy the first card. How does that sound?"

She was as thrilled as could be and asked, "Can we go now?"

"Yes, Sue, we can go now."

I have always lived on a budget and certainly didn't have money falling out of my pockets, so I quickly surveyed the display windows and pointed to the phones that I could afford.

She looked at all the affordable phones and picked the one she wanted. She loved her phone and thanked me over and over. You'd think I'd just bought her a brand-new car! However, that was not the last phone I would buy for her. She either lost, broke, dropped, or had multiple phones stolen.

Eventually, to keep her phone safe and hidden, she ripped a piece of the lining in her oversized purse and tucked her phone underneath the fabric at the bottom of her bag. Her phone was her lifeline and her security. Oh, did Sue ever love her phone!

Do You Know a Sue?

One day, I heard my phone ringing and looked at the clock. It was two o'clock in the morning. No one likes to hear their phone ringing at that hour. I picked it up and heard a police officer say, "Hello, are you Wendy Shelley?"

"Yes, I am," I said in a shaky voice, with fear gnawing at my stomach. Middle-of-the-night phone calls are terrifying for anyone.

The officer proceeded, "Do you know a Sue?" and continued with her last name.

"Yes, yes, I do," I replied as I sat up in bed and struggled to wake up.

"Sue tells me you are her next of kin? Is that true?"

Startled with that unbelievable revelation again, I replied, "Yes, yes, I am." I wondered what was coming next. She couldn't have been in a car accident because she didn't drive. *Oh no, what's happened to her?* I thought.

The officer continued. "A concerned citizen called the police when they noticed a female staggering onto the street and into traffic. She seems to be high on something, so I drove her home. I asked her if I could call anyone for her, and she gave me your number. She wanted you to know she is okay and she'll call you in the morning."

I thanked the female officer for contacting me, and asked her to tell Sue that I was glad she was okay and that I would talk to her tomorrow.

My dear Sue. She wanted the officer to call me because she needed to know that someone in this world cared whether she lived or died. *Oh Lord,* I prayed aloud, *Sue is so alone and lost. Help me to find a way to bring her to You.*

Card Experiment

A well-known card company decided to donate Mother's Day cards to a prison, allowing inmates to send their mothers cards for Mother's Day. A month before that special day, the card company set up a booth for inmates to choose a card and send it in the mail. It was a great success, and they assured the inmates that they would be back next year.

When Father's Day rolled around, they came again, expecting the same positive results. However, the vendor was in for a shock. There were so few inmates who wanted Father's Day cards that the company decided it just wasn't worth their while to ever come back.

When I read that story, my heart was saddened. Clearly, prisons are full of people with the same disadvantage as Sue: an absent father. Without a dad's support, often children have nowhere to turn and don't know what to do when life gets to be too much to handle.

Sue didn't understand what a good father was, so she struggled to even fathom a kind heavenly Father. I talked about God in the plainest of terms to her, usually with a simple, "God loves you, Sue." With her tainted view of fatherhood, it was difficult to comprehend a God that would love and care about her. Unmistakably, a whole family suffers when a father is gone, as was evidenced in this card experiment, and as proved to be true in Sue's life.

However, all is not lost for those without caring dads. Our kind heavenly Father is a perfect Father, and His word promises, "He heals the brokenhearted and binds up their wounds" (Psalm 147:3 NIV).

If the truth were known, God has been interested in our individual lives since our very beginning, our conception really. Listen to what the Psalmist says:

You made all the delicate, inner parts of my body and knit me together in my mother's womb. Thank you for making me so wonderfully complex! Your workmanship is marvelous—how well I know it. You watched me as I was being formed in utter seclusion, as I was woven together in the dark of the womb. You saw me before I was born. Every day of my life was recorded in your book. Every moment was laid out before a single day had passed. How precious are your thoughts about me, O God. They cannot be numbered! I can't even count them;

they outnumber the grains of sand! And when I wake up, you are still with me! (Psalm 139:13–19 NLT)

What a beautiful truth: God's eye has been on each one of us long before we took our first breath. My sent-for-one assignment was sent by God to tell Sue how much He cared for her. However, today, perhaps you need to hear the same certainty as well: God loves and cares for you.

CHAPTER 6

It Costs to Love

Breakfast—and a Little Bit More!

Sue moved again and gave me her address. When I pulled up to the building, even the entrance looked scary to me—I wasn't about to go knocking on that dilapidated door. Thankfully, Sue appeared right on time, smiling. She knew I'd come, and off we went for breakfast.

There was a nice breakfast cafe close by, and I opted to take her there. She always stuck close to me when we were out in public. She reminded me of a tourist, always looking around and taking in all their surroundings. The restaurant was quite crowded that morning; however, there was one table vacant, so we sat there.

I gave her the menu and told her to order anything she wanted. She handed it back. Embarrassed, she said in a raspy whisper, "I don't read well. What do they serve here?"

I proceeded to read off some of the breakfasts, and as per usual, she ordered the works: pancakes, bacon, sausage, eggs, toast—everything! I wondered how her little body could consume such quantities. No problem, though, Sue always cleaned her plate, and I liked knowing she was well nourished.

After we finished, I got up to pay, and left her sitting at the table. The waitress came to the cash register, and I handed her the bill. As I reached in my purse for my wallet, I happened to glance back in the direction of our table, just in time to see Sue scooping all the jams and honey containers from the table dispenser, into her open purse on her knee.

"Thirteen ninety-five, please," the waitress said.

I turned back to the waitress and looked like a deer in headlights. I hadn't heard a word she said.

"Thirteen ninety-five, ma'am?"

"Oh yes, okay," I muttered, and I handed her the money.

I went back to our table, and Sue smiled as if nothing had happened. I was horrified. I didn't know what to do. *Do I confront her? Tell her it's wrong to steal? Do I make her put them back? Or do I go to the waitress and pay for the jams and honey she stole?* I was internally debating. I stood there flabbergasted and had a split second to decide. I thought, *I can't confront her here, in front of everyone. I just can't do it.* Truthfully, I just wanted to be out of the restaurant.

I drove back to her place, and she didn't say a word about the incident. When she hopped out of my truck, she was as happy as can be: her belly was full, and her purse—well, it was jam packed, literally! The next time I went to that restaurant, I randomly left extra money to cover the stolen condiments. Whether I did the right thing or not, I still don't know. At least I paid for what she stole and felt better that the restaurant wasn't out the money.

I've learned throughout life that unstable people do unstable things. Disturbed people do the same: disturbing things. As I spent more time with Sue, I saw more cracks in her thought processes. She didn't have a sound mind to make the best decisions.

Battered and Bruised

This is the saddest part of Sue's story, and I won't stay here long. Sue was always skittish and never lost that jitter. She reminded me of a cowering animal, ducking and weaving, always afraid of the next blow.

During our visits throughout the years, something would trigger a painful memory of the past, and haunting thoughts would batter her mind. To be honest, listening to her recall incidents of heartbreak was just that: heartbreaking. I've blanked out of my mind most of our conversations, simply because I have to. I cannot dwell on such cruelties.

I was at the shopping mall one day when my phone buzzed, and it was Sue. I always answered her calls. "Sue, Sue, slow down, Sue," I said. As I listened to her fast, high-pitched voice, she wasn't making any sense. "What are you saying, Sue? What's happened?"

I pieced together the horrific story she was describing and will intentionally be vague because of the extreme cruelty of this incident. From what I could gather, she was at a girlfriend's house the night before doing cocaine, but the girlfriend wasn't there. Since it was summertime and a Friday night, the girlfriend was out on the town in the packed bars. When the girlfriend returned, she called Sue outside to say a couple of friends were waiting with free drugs for her. Of course that couldn't be true, but when you're an addict, anything free is tantalizing. Unbelievably, her girlfriend betrayed her to a low-life bunch from the bar, in exchange for merely a few dollars. Sue doesn't remember how long she laid in the alley beside her girlfriend's place, but when she came to long enough to figure out her surroundings, she dragged herself back to her apartment, alone, with a broken body, and like so many other times in her life, a shattered and wounded heart.

The next day, I took the time and went to see her. She was so battered and bruised, it was shocking. Both her eyes were swollen with yellow bruises forming in their sockets, and her dear little face already turning a light purple from indiscriminate smacks, and both her arms were covered in black and blue bruises. "Oh, my goodness, gracious," I whispered under my breath, "I've never seen anyone beaten like this." I couldn't believe my eyes. *Oh, dear Jesus.*

I darted toward her and held her close, stroking her golden hair, trying to ease her agony. I was only five years older than Sue, but throughout our whole friendship, I assumed her much-needed role: that of a loving, caring mother. My poor little Sue; she had suffered so much in her life, and I felt so terribly sorry for her.

I whispered as we embraced, "Sue, bad men do bad things. I'm so sorry, Sue. I'm just so sorry."

More Moving Around

Another time, I heard the phone ringing and answered. I learned that Sue was moving again.

"Oh Sue, why? You've only been in your own place a few months. You know it's best to stay by yourself."

"I know, Wendy, but it's cheaper to share a place than to pay the full rent myself; it will work out," Sue replied. But I knew better. It never worked out that way, not for Sue.

I parked in front of the address she gave me and sat in the car, waiting for her to appear. I called her cell phone, and there was no answer. This was the only day and the only time I could spare this week. I thought that if I got out of the car, she would see me through a window, but that wasn't the case.

Now what do I do? I thought. I knew I was at the right place, as Sue had pointed out this shabby building to me before. A guy she knew lived there, and she moved in with him. I could see the apartment number over a small door around the side, but I didn't feel good about walking in-between two buildings. It was just a little too creepy for me.

Ten minutes passed, and Sue still hadn't come. *Should I stay or should I go?* I thought. I stood around for a few more minutes and then made an instant decision to bolt toward the door and knock loudly. Quickly, I stepped back several steps within clear sight of the road. I heard voices inside, so Sue must have heard me. *Good,* I thought. *I hope she comes quickly.* I backed up closer toward the road and waited. Sure enough, out Sue came smiling—with her friend right behind her.

I got my first glimpse of this guy. He was old, much older than her. He looked scruffy and scary, which most of her friends did, and he was quite tall, with worn-out clothes hanging over his thin body. I was reluctant to meet her male friends; I was an obvious outsider and always felt uncomfortable.

Be smart, Wendy, I said to myself. *Keep backing up. You've never seen this guy before. Don't engage in any conversation. You're in a back alley. Keep moving toward the road.* I kept walking backward, and he kept walking toward me. *Oh no,* I thought. *Stop. Stop walking toward me!*

He held out his hand to shake mine, and before I could say a word, he said, "I wanted to meet you. Sue's told me so much about you."

"Oh," I replied, startled. I hadn't expected such a warmhearted greeting. I shook his hand and smiled slightly, making sure I was within clear sight of the road. With a quicker release than I normally would, I took another step back, wanting to keep a lot of space between us. "Nice to meet you, as well. Sue's my friend."

I Beg Your Pardon?

"Are you ready, Sue?" I asked, and gestured for her to come with me. I didn't like standing in this alley. However, he jumped in with a question.

He smiled warmly and asked, "Where did you come from, actually?"

My brow furrowed. What was he talking about, where did I come from? I didn't have a clue what he meant.

"Excuse me?" I asked with eyebrows raised, very skeptical of where he was going with this question.

"Where did you come from?" he asked again, and I still had no idea what he was talking about. Did he mean where was I born? Or what nationality I was? Did he mean what town I lived in? I didn't know what he was getting at.

"Pardon?" I asked again, puzzled.

He continued, "Sue's told me you help her, you love her, and you are kind. I've never heard of anyone like you—you must be an angel."

I nervously laughed and shook my head. "Oh no, no, no—an angel?—oh my goodness no, I'm not an angel. I'm very much a human being, I'm just Sue's friend."

"Yes, I know that," he said with the utmost sincerity, "but why do you care about her? I don't understand why you help her. Who are you? Where did you come from?"

To fill in the awkward silence, because I was standing there speechless, he continued, "Angels help people. You must be an angel." For a minute, I thought he was joking and was about to laugh, but the seriousness on his face revealed otherwise. He was asking in all honesty: who was I?

"Oh, no, no, no," I said again, shaking my head as I spoke, "I help Sue because I love Jesus, and God sent me to her."

Next, he replied in a serious tone, and I've never forgotten how he looked, or how his voice sounded when he said, "Then where do I find a Wendy like you? An angel like you? Someone sent from God to help me?"

I stood there, and no words came out. What do you say to that? How do you respond? I just looked at him and didn't know what to say. I couldn't answer his question because I simply didn't have an answer. The reason that I did what I did was because of my love for my Savior, the Lord Jesus Christ. Pure and simple. I was a pencil in God's hand, and that was all.

A moment slipped by, and I kindly replied, "Jesus loves you. He cares for you, like He cares for Sue, and today, God sent me here to tell you, as well—Jesus loves and cares for you."

He smiled and stretched out his hand again. "Thank you. Thank you." He said very warmly, "It's very nice to meet you."

I returned the handshake this time and didn't release quite as fast. "God bless you. Jesus loves you."

I never saw that man again. The following year, he succumbed to his addictions and died. I did wonder, though, did our brief exchange cause him to think about angels, to think about a God who loved him? The Bible says that God is not willing that any should perish, and because God is so merciful, He creates countless opportunities for people to hear about Him. I hope he made his peace with God before he drew his last breath; I sure hope so.

It Truly Costs to Love

Out of necessity, Sue stuffed her emotions where they could not be found—except, unbeknownst to her, God knows every hiding place. He was beginning to soften her heart, and love was doing it.

David and I regularly say to each other, "It costs to love." It sounds like a simple principle, but to put it into practice requires great perseverance and personal sacrifice. Over the course of our lives, we have learned that to love others with all your heart requires you to give of yourself, to give of your time, and to give of your resources. And the more extravagant your love, the more it simply will cost you. The Lord Jesus Christ is our perfect example: He loved so deeply that He gave the ultimate "more" and laid down His life for all of humanity. He is our model of perfect love.

Maybe you have been loving a hard-nosed spouse for a long time, or a wayward child; perhaps you have been caring for a sick loved one or helping a confused grandchild, or maybe you are loving a friend like Sue, and today, the cost seems overwhelming. Love, really, in and of itself, is an unselfish act extended by you to another human being, regardless of how they act or how they look. God's word says, "Love never fails," and I believe that truth wholeheartedly.

Sue Is Softening

Despite everything Sue had endured in life, she never blamed God. She felt she was just born on the wrong side of the tracks and therefore, was simply unlucky. It is a good perspective really: it bothers me when people blame God for everything because God is good and has never made a mistake. It is the enemy who is out to kill, steal, and destroy, and our anger should be fully directed at him.

One day Sue told me, "Wendy, if I had been raised like you, I'd be good like you."

I smiled. "I know, Sue. I'm sorry you had to raise yourself and your life has been so hard. It's God that makes the difference in anyone's life, and it is only God that makes us good."

"I should have died many times over," she said. "Maybe God protected me?"

"He sure did, Sue. God protected you so our paths would cross, so I could tell you God loves you." The Psalms records David as saying, in Psalm 27:10, "When my father and my mother forsake me, then the Lord will take care of me" (NKJV). Even though Sue went through many hardships, and was certainly forsaken by just about everyone, the Lord did take care of her by allowing our paths to cross.

Sue saw Christ in me, but she didn't know it was Him. She saw His reflection in my face but gave me the credit. Even when we give our best for God, the Bible says it is still like filthy rags when compared to the Lord Jesus Christ and the best He gave—which was Himself on the cross for our sins. We can never equate our human goodness to God's goodness—it's simply not a match. This special assignment was all God's idea—my being sent-for-one.

Chapter 7

Scared to Death

The Flipside, Once Again!

I was standing beside Sue at the front desk of the Salvation Army when the volunteer asked me, "May I see your Christmas voucher, please?"

"My Christmas voucher?" I answered with surprise. "Oh no, no, I'm not here for anything. I'm just here with my friend."

"Oh, okay," she said matter-of-factly. "No problem. Just go through those doors."

That day, I had driven Sue to the Salvation Army for extra kitchen staples: flour, pasta, soups, and whatever else was available. Since it was November and close to Christmas, the room was full of generous donations—hand-knit hats and mittens, scarfs, sweaters, blankets, and all kinds of items. Because Sue didn't have to walk back to her apartment, she was able to stock up with extra things she needed. God bless the Salvation Army; what a blessing they have been to millions of people.

Sue showed the volunteer her Christmas voucher and hastily went through the double doors behind me. We walked down a short hallway, and as we entered the large gymnasium where the rectangular tables were set up around the perimeter with all the donated goods, Sue had to show another volunteer her voucher, one more time.

Oh no! I thought. *Not that silly voucher again!*

This time, I gestured for Sue to go first. The lady looked at Sue's voucher and motioned for her to go inside the gymnasium. I followed close behind and not even looking up, attempted to skoosh in behind Sue to avoid the voucher question; but my plan failed, and the lady called me back.

"Excuse me, miss, may I see your voucher before you proceed any further?"

No! I thought to myself. *I don't have a voucher! I donate to the Salvation Army, and it's very likely my donations are here!*

I smiled politely. "I'm not here for anything, actually. I'm just here with my friend."

She questioned me, "So you don't need anything?"

"No, no. I don't need anything." But I had to ask myself, *How is it that I am mistaken for being on the flipside, again and again?* Humbling, to say the least.

As I watched numerous people gather the things they needed for the Christmas season, I couldn't help but recall the words of Jesus:

I was a stranger and you did not invite me in, I needed clothes and you did not clothe me, I was sick and in prison and you did not look after me. They also will answer, "Lord, when did we see you hungry or thirsty or a stranger or needing clothes or sick or in prison, and did not help you?" He will reply, "Truly I tell you, whatever you did not do for one of the least of these, you did not do for me." (Matthew 25:43–45 NIV)

Sue, and all the others at the Salvation Army that day, were literally one of the, "least of these" referred to in that scripture. When we help those in need in any way—by knitting, sewing, cooking, volunteering, caring, or giving—Jesus says we are doing such acts of kindness for Him. Quite a profound thought, really.

Please Come, Wendy—Fast!

About six years into our friendship, Sue called me one day to say she was moving to the country.

"Who in the world do you know in the country, Sue?" I asked.

Sue mentioned a guy who lived in an apartment attached to the back of a house; she said she was moving in with him. "Oh, Sue," I said, "remember our talk? You are best to live by yourself. It's never good when you move in with people. Did you have to give up your apartment? Oh, Sue. You have my number. Please call me if you need me."

After a few weeks of living in this new spot, Sue did call me one afternoon. As I recall now, it was late November, and whispering into her cell phone, Sue said, "Can you come and get me?"

"Sue, what's the matter? Where are you?" I asked.

"I had to leave, Wendy. I couldn't stay another day. I'm on road number nine just before the bridge. Please bring me a coat. I had to run out, and I didn't grab a thing."

I asked no further questions and replied, "Okay, I'll come right now."

Fortunately, I was home that afternoon and could slip out. I grabbed my keys, found an extra winter coat that belonged to one of my daughters, and quickly got in my car to find her. *Road number nine, just before the bridge. Which side?* I wondered. *Left or right? Oh, dear Jesus, help me to find this place and to find her!*

I Spot Her

I traveled along the country road, and each time a car approached from behind, I pulled my car over to let them pass. I needed to go slower than the traffic as I didn't want to miss her. Suddenly, way off in the distance, I thought I could see a change in the road's landscape and hoped I was close to the bridge. As I drew closer, I spotted a lone figure on the side of the road. *Could that be Sue?* I wondered.

Yes, that's her, I said to myself, but I couldn't believe my eyes. Sue was standing there on this cold day, clothed only in a thin shirt and jogging pants—no purse, no nothing—just watching for me. *Oh Jesus,* I cried aloud, *she trusts me so much!*

I pulled over, grabbed the winter coat I brought, and jumped out of the car. "Sue, oh Sue! You're frozen." I wrapped the coat around her and opened the car door, and she got in. I turned up the heat as high as it would go, and Sue sat there with her teeth chattering and shivering uncontrollably, shaking like a leaf on this cold, early winter day.

"I knew you would come, Wendy," she whispered. "I just knew you would come." Tears flooded my eyes as I readjusted the heating vents and turned them fully toward her. *What if I hadn't been home? Or had just run outside and missed her call?*

Sue continued, "I'm sorry to have called you, Wendy, but I was frantic. I just couldn't stay. He's a crazy man, and I was scared to death. There was no way I could get to town unless you drove me. I couldn't walk, and I have no money for a taxi."

"That's okay, Sue," I assured her. "I'm glad I was home when you called."

After she spent a few more minutes describing her harrowing experience, I spoke up. "You must be hungry. Let's go to town and get some food and we'll talk."

Interestingly, in all the years I knew her, God never asked me to take her into my home. He allowed me to keep those two worlds separate, and to be honest—I was thankful. God was loving her through me, on her turf, and that was my assignment.

After Sue thawed out and a good warm meal was in her tummy, she handed me a paper with another address. She asked, "Can you take me to this address?"

I found this to be her sad routine. She would stay with a friend for a little while and then get her own place again. If she spent too much money on drugs and cigarettes, and didn't save enough for rent, eventually, she would get evicted and have to move again. The same merry-go-round took place when she had her own apartment. Then her place became the revolving door. What a miserable existence, always moving around and never belonging anywhere.

Eternal Life in Heaven

In those early years, I wondered if my assignment included not only loving Sue but bringing her to Jesus. *But how in the world would that ever happen?* I thought to myself. *She's about as lost as anyone I've ever seen. How do I tell a drug addict, who's frequently high, that she needs to accept Christ as her Savior?* It seemed almost impossible.

However, I started to pray, "Lord, show me a way to tell Sue about you in a way she would understand." I knew I was meeting her practical needs, but how on earth would I be able to meet her spiritual need? I had no clue—other than just to love her and tell her that God loves her even more.

Sue understood she was a sinner, that was for sure; however, like so many others, Sue thought when you died, you went to a "better place" regardless of how you lived on earth. I can certainly see where that thought would bring a sense of comfort and relief, but according to the Bible, that notion is simply not true.

Jesus said, "I am the way, the truth, and the life. No one comes to the Father except through Me" (John 14:6 NKJV). Therefore, the way to Father God is through His one and only Son: the Lord Jesus. *Show me a way. Oh Lord, please show me a way for Sue to understand who You are.*

Scared to Death

When Sue abruptly fled the country apartment with only the clothes on her back, she wanted to return and gather the few possessions she left behind.

"Wendy, I need to get my things. Will you drive me back to the apartment so I can get my stuff?" she asked.

"Sue, I will have to talk to David and see when he can take us. It's too unsafe for us to go ourselves. I will talk to him and get back to you."

I spoke to my husband, and he agreed to accompany us out to this country place. "Sure, tell Sue we will pick her up and go there tomorrow, late afternoon, right before supper."

My husband parked outside of Sue's current place, and we waited for her to appear. At the appointed time, Sue came out the door and quickly hopped in the car. Normally, Sue loved car rides; however, this ride wasn't going to be fun, and she was notably nervous.

We traveled the ten minutes out of town and came to the house before the bridge on road number nine. David turned into the driveway, and to be honest, I was a bit surprised. It looked like a nice property. There was a winding driveway meandering up a gradual incline, and even in the winter with the russet-colored ground and leafless trees, it looked like a decent place.

However, Sue told us to go past the main house and around the back and to the right. As we turned, there was an attached steel shed, jutting out about twenty feet from the back of the house. "The apartment is through that door," Sue said.

I looked and thought, *Through that door?*

My husband parked the car on an angle right by the shed door and kept his driver's window fully rolled down. I had no idea what I was getting myself into, and I wanted him to hear me if I yelled.

I'd been to creepy places with Sue before, but this shed looked about as dilapidated and scary as I had ever seen. She opened the graying, stiff, steel shed door by giving it a shake with both hands, and then we proceeded to go inside. I trailed close behind her, not even wanting to look to the left or right. This place was ominous. With each step, I felt fear wash over me like a shower.

I stepped over open boxes, some of them half-filled with tools and other random stuff, while other boxes spilled over with what appeared to be junk. Then, there was broken glass in old window frames and a crumbled piece of steel thrown on top of other boxes, which I suppose was once a screen door. I saw green garbage bags thrown all over, which I'm assuming contained trash—you could smell the nasty, rotting garbage—and then, add the stale odor of the musty shed. The whole place was disgusting, and we hadn't even made it to the apartment door.

Sue hurried toward a dark brown door that was straight ahead, with her shoulders stooped forward and her head bowed low. Once again, like so many other times in her life, she was trying to muster up enough courage for what lay beyond another apartment door.

Sue knocked loudly and then opened the door and shouted boldly in a curt, no-nonsense, brave voice, "I'm here to get my things!" But I knew she was scared to death, and I must admit, I was, as well.

I stood in the doorway, too afraid to move. The person Sue described as the crazy man was sitting at the kitchen table. He was unshaven, with a cigarette dangling between two fingers and a beer bottle cupped securely in the other hand. He was clearly inebriated, and when he saw Sue, he slurred a few words but I couldn't make out what he was saying—and I doubt Sue could understand him either.

The whole scene before me was simply unbelievable. *She lived here? With this guy?* The thought sickened me. I just couldn't believe my eyes. I'm surprised she lasted a month.

He certainly didn't expect to see someone coming in behind Sue, but thankfully, he didn't react to my presence.

Sue scurried as fast as a mouse, quickly looking for her things and throwing them in a green garbage bag. I stood in the doorway with my heart beating out of my chest.

After taking a long drag on his cigarette and blowing the smoke high in the air, he laid the smoldering butt in a saucer on the table and turned to the right to see what Sue was doing. *His elbow is awfully close to the saucer,* I thought to myself. *He's going to light his shirt on fire!*

I quickly scanned the room. The space was maybe twenty-five square feet, covered in dark brownish paneling. In one corner was a small apartment-sized stove and an equally small fridge. There was a short countertop heaped with dirty dishes, and in front of the counter was a mossy green–colored rectangular table, with two wooden chairs. This was, I assumed, the "kitchen." In another corner was an unmade bed, with blankets crumbled in the middle, and in the far-left corner, shockingly, was a cotton curtain hanging from the ceiling to the floor, separating the "bathroom" from everything else. This was truly a one-room shack.

I stood there stunned and speechless. He looked up from the table; my eyes locked with his, but I quickly looked away. This was not the time, nor the place, to engage in a conversation with this man.

Luckily, Sue moved with lightning speed, and when it appeared she had retrieved all her belongings, she rushed toward me. I quickly turned and took a step out the door, with her right behind me. Neither of us could get out of that place fast enough. We hopped in the car and quickly tumbled into our seats. We made it out, unscathed. Yikes. That was something else!

A few months after Sue left this shed apartment, I read in the newspaper that the entire house burned to the ground—and if I was to speculate, the fire likely started in that one-room shack.

I'm Moving

My husband and I had talked of selling our farm and relocating closer to where he worked. A move like this meant that I would be a one-hour drive, one way, from Sue. The thought of telling her I would be moving made me nauseous. I promised myself, as I did when she moved from her first apartment, that I wouldn't abandon her. I prayed and asked God to help her understand I was moving away.

Once our farm sold, I had to tell her. I called Sue to say I would pick her up for lunch and take her to McDonalds. I thought to myself, *I'll tell her while she is wolfing down a meal: maybe that will make it easier?*

After she ordered her food and sat down, I knew I had to get this conversation over with, so I began. "Sue, remember my husband commutes into the city each day?"

"Yes," she replied, not looking up as she munched on her double bacon cheeseburger.

I cleared my throat. I'm not sure why we do this when we're about to make a contentious statement. Nonetheless, I continued, "It's too far for him to travel every day. We decided to sell our farm and move closer to his work." There, I said it—albeit nervously.

She looked up with raised eyebrows, and not allowing any lull in the conversation, I continued hastily. "I want you to know, I'll come back and see you once a month and bring you groceries. You have your cell phone, so we can talk, and if you need me, I'll just be an hour away. You are my friend, and I love you. I won't leave you, Sue. I won't abandon you, I promise!"

I was rambling anxiously, because her face revealed a blank stare. Sue stopped eating and looked me straight in the eyes. *Oh no!* I thought.

"Okay, Wendy," she began, "You are my best friend, and I know you'll come back when you say. That is okay. I understand. I love you." And that was it. She grabbed her burger and finished it off.

Her faith in me was so overwhelming that even now as I write her story, I still shake my head in disbelief. She trusted me so much, and even more humbling was God's faith in me. He trusted me with this assignment and kept me going back and back—never giving up on this one soul.

I really should not have been surprised at Sue's reaction to the news of our move; I had asked God to help her understand, and that's exactly what He did. It was God who was writing Sue's story. It was His love story for one, and as Mother Theresa said so honorably, "I was simply the pencil."

I continued to make the one-hour trek every third week of the month for many years. I would call a day ahead, and Sue would be ready with her needed list. To be honest, I really didn't think she would live much past a year or two, so I didn't foresee my driving back and forth would continue for any significant length of time.

Wow, was I in for a surprise! I would have never dreamed at the time of our move that my sent-for-one assignment would continue for another dozen years!

Chapter 8

Sue's Surprises

Do You Celebrate Christmas?

This was the question I asked Sue the first year of our friendship.

She looked at me and slowly said, "No, I don't celebrate anything."

"Well this year, Sue, things will be different. To celebrate Christmas, I'll bring you a Christmas present."

Just before Christmas, I climbed the two flights of stairs in the smoky stairwell, stood in front of her thin, hollow apartment door, and knocked.

"Who is it?" Sue snarled.

"It's Wendy, Sue! Remember? I called and told you I was coming today?" Once she knew it was me behind the door, she always changed her tone of voice; it's as if she turned on a "nice" switch. She opened the door with a smile, and I held out her package. "This is for you, Sue. Merry Christmas!" Her eyes grew big as she reached up to receive her gift.

"For me?" she asked.

"For you!" I responded.

Sue sat on the ratty cloth couch, while I sat on my favorite wooden chair by the door, always with my coat and shoes on. Sue slowly and carefully unwrapped her present, almost like the gradual unfurling of a delicate rose. There was no question in my mind that Sue had not received a gift in a very long time, and she was savoring the moment. I decided on a housecoat and slippers that first year and wrapped them in the best paper I could find with a giant bow.

She opened her gift, and for a fleeting moment, love melted an addict's tough exterior. Sue stood to her feet, put her housecoat over her clothes, and slipped her feet into the cozy slippers. She looked at me with the warmest eyes possible and said, "Thank you so much." Her reaction to this random act of kindness made me think, *I need to continue blessing Sue at Christmastime.*

My Young Son Meets Sue

It was the Saturday before Christmas during the second year of our friendship, and my then ten-year-old son, Josiah, came with me to bring Sue Christmas. I discovered in a few previous conversations that Sue would happily cook a meal for special occasions but just never had the extra money to buy the necessary food. So, we brought all the fixings to cook a turkey dinner, along with her gifts.

We arrived at Sue's building and made our way to the exterior door, carrying her gift and a box of Christmas food. Just before we went inside the creepy stairwell, I leaned over and whispered to my son, "The lady we are going to visit is my friend. She doesn't have anyone to buy her a Christmas present, so we bought her one. Plus, she needs a little food. Sue doesn't live like we do, son, but she needs our help."

We walked up the dimly lit staircase with Josiah carrying Sue's present, and with each step we took, his eyes grew bigger and bigger. To this ten-year-old boy, this was about the scariest place he had ever seen. We stood at her door and knocked. Josiah had never even smelled a place like this before, let alone been in a building such as this. I smiled and said softly, "It's okay, son. We won't stay long."

Sue opened the door and welcomed us into her apartment. She was so happy to see me and to meet one of my children. Josiah followed me mechanically, saying absolutely nothing. After setting the bags down on Sue's table and presenting her with her Christmas gift, I quickly reached for Josiah's hand and held it secure. I knew by the look on Josiah's face that he was in quiet shock. He stood beside me, not moving a muscle. He had never seen a mess like this in his life. Sue's place always looked like a tornado had ripped through.

I made idle conversation for a couple of minutes and then told Sue we needed to be going. She thanked us and said goodbye, and we made our way down the stairs. Josiah held on to my hand in this tight, vice-grip kind of grasp and never let go until we were safely back in the car.

Interestingly, Sue never forgot meeting this little boy of mine and talked about this encounter for the rest of her life; and just as interesting, my son has too.

Sue's Excited!

Now in the third year of our friendship, December rolled around again, and I parked in front of Sue's rundown building. I had gathered her Christmas presents and a box containing a turkey and all the trimmings and made my way up the stairs to her second-floor apartment. Even during the day, and after coming here for several years already, my heart quickened as the stairwell closed in on me. I knocked on her door, and immediately she opened it wide. Right away, I noticed something different. She was excited—like, unusually excited!

I brought in her things; however, she paid no attention at all to my load. *Hmmm,* I thought, *she's acting very odd and I'm not feeling comfortable. I wonder what she's up to.* I was always on guard when I was in this apartment building.

"Wait here!" she said as she disappeared into her bedroom.

"A Gift for Me?"

I could hear her shuffling about, and then Sue reappeared with a present. It was all wrapped the best she could, with the best she had. I had never expected a gift from her, or ever wanted one, and she caught me quite by surprise.

"Wendy, I want to give this to you. I want you to have it." And with sheer delight, she handed me a gift. I knew she couldn't afford a present like this, and I didn't know quite what to say.

"Open it, open it!" Sue said excitedly.

I sat down on the hard, wooden chair and slowly removed the wrapping paper. As I pulled the paper back to reveal its contents, I immediately knew what it was.

"It's mine!" she said. "I've had it for a long time, and I want to give it to you." She was on the edge of her seat with her hands clasped in front of her chest, waiting for my approval.

My present was a keepsake porcelain doll, the kind you display on shelves and buy in specialty shops. The doll was about eighteen inches high and in its original packaging. Clearly, it was the most expensive thing she owned, and it looked like it had never been removed from the box.

"Sue," I exclaimed, "it's so beautiful! I love it. This must be very special to you. Thank you so much."

"It is very special, and you are the only one I want to give it to. I know you'll treasure it."

Her actions remind me of a verse in the Bible that says, "It is more blessed to give than to receive" (Acts 20:35 NKJV), and without even knowing this principle, Sue was experiencing the joy of giving, and the added bliss of giving her best!

Fast-forward to the next year's Christmas, and when I came in with Sue's present, again, she disappeared to her bedroom. A few moments later she reappeared, bubbling over with joy. She was yet again holding another present, all wrapped like the Christmas before. I opened the box, and it was another treasured doll!

"Wendy, I only have two of these special dolls, and I saved this one for you for this Christmas."

I had no idea how long she had them or where they came from. I loved this little lady, and now, she was beginning to love me back the best way she knew how.

Bigger Gifts!

It is now the next Christmas, and she came out with an even bigger box than the two times before! I wondered to myself what the contents were, as the Christmas before she had given me her last doll.

"Open it, open it!" she said eagerly, just like last time.

This box was newer than the last two, and when I opened it, here lay another beautiful keepsake doll, more exquisite than the other two—and this one was brand new.

"Sue, it's so beautiful! I love it!" I exclaimed, though all the while I am wondering where she found the gift and where did she get the money for it, as I knew these unique keepsake dolls cost hundreds of dollars!

As if she was reading my mind, Sue said proudly, "I bought it in January."

With a wrinkled brow, I asked, "January? You mean this past January, eleven months ago?"

"Yes," she said, beaming. "I sent in payments every month all year. Once they received the last payment, they sent me the doll."

I sat there stunned. Her purchasing this gift for me on a payment plan was simply unbelievable. She giggled with joy as I carefully inspected her gift.

I was so taken aback to receive another treasure from her. I remember thinking that day, *Lord Jesus, may I never let Sue down. Help me to be faithful to the assignment You have given me, and may she never be disappointed in You because of me.*

The following year, Sue bought me yet another keepsake doll, on the same payment plan, bringing the grand total to four unique dolls! Today, I have them displayed on a shelf in my home, right where I'm writing her story. Such a reminder of extravagant giving—Sue gave me her very best.

Christmas for Sue—a Family Event

I had known Sue for so long that my children grew up and became adults. After nearly a dozen years into my friendship with Sue, my oldest daughter, Tennille, suggested to her four siblings that they forego their Christmas gift-giving to each other and assist me with blessing Sue. My other children heartily agreed. "Christmas for Sue" was now going to be a family event.

In November of each year, Sue gave me a list of items she needed, and together, we bought all on the list—and more. Not only did we buy gifts, but we made up food hampers as well. Even my children's children got involved; I remember popping into my son Gabriel's home one day, and one of his little boys came running toward me carrying a nicely wrapped gift and said, "We bought this for Sue! Can you give this to Sue for Christmas?" He had no idea who Sue was but had heard his parents talk about buying a gift for a lady named Sue who needed a little extra help.

Now my children were teaching *their* children the joy of giving to others—and not just others who can give them a gift back, but teaching them to give their best to the poor, someone less fortunate than them, and someone they may never, ever meet.

Sue began to love all my family and kept their Christmas photo cards taped to her kitchen cabinet all year. When I would visit her, she would point to the pictures and say, "These are my children too."

"Yes, they are Sue, and they love you."

Fourteen years into our friendship, one of my grown daughters, Vanessa, came with me to bring Sue Christmas. We brought in five big hampers of food and another box of gifts. My daughter still recalls that afternoon.

Vanessa remembers Sue's place looking bare, with yellowy, mustard-colored walls and hardly a picture hanging anywhere. She remembers the strong cigarette smell, like nothing she'd ever smelt before. There was a single couch along the long living room wall and a coffee table in front of the couch. A television took up the corner space, and then there was Sue's little bed off to one side. By this time, Sue's health had become quite poor, forcing her to be bedridden for much of the time. In the eating area, there was a Christmas tree all decorated and waiting for our gifts and a lone kitchen table with four chairs in the middle of the room.

Vanessa recalls being surprised at Sue's small stature. With so many addictions wearing out her physical body, Sue was so tiny, looking so much older than her age.

Sue hugged us both and with tears in her eyes said, "Thank you, thank you so much!" For Sue to tear up was quite unusual, as long ago, she had placed her emotions under lock and key.

Sue was very happy to have met Vanessa. Now, she had a grown-up face to the children she called her own, by proxy.

"Your family is my family," she told me, and I always agreed.

Sorrowfully, Sue did have her own biological children; however, because of her addictions, she was unable to care for them properly, and they were all taken away by the Children's Aid Society. As the years ticked by, buried deep within her heart where Sue stuffed her emotions to survive, lay a bed of bitter regret and sadness at being such a neglectful, addicted mother.

Jail Time

One Saturday afternoon after we had moved away, around the eighth year of our friendship, my phone rang.

"Wendy," Sue said in a complete panic, "I'm in jail. Please come and get me out of here. I hate this place! The people are wild, and I'm scared to death."

"Sue, what are you talking about? You're in jail? Where are you?" I asked.

Sue was so frightened and continued, "We were all doing crack and got busted. They arrested everyone and brought me here, but Wendy, I can't stay here, I just can't! I'm in a cell with crazy people. Can you come? I have to get out of here!"

"Of course, I'll come, but Sue, I can't bust you out! I'll call the jail and see if I can come tomorrow, but I don't know how the system works. Call me back this time tomorrow, and I'll see what I can do. Jesus loves you, Sue, and He is with you. You need to pray to God."

She replied, "I have been. I'm so scared."

We've talked about this scenario dozens of times, and Sue always nodded her head in agreement. "You can't go where people are doing bad things. It makes *you* do bad things. You have to stay away!" Of course, that's easy for anyone to say—but like everyone, easy to say and hard to do.

I didn't know one thing about jails, but I did know the culprit behind everyone's jail time. The Bible tells us clearly, "Be sober, be vigilant; because your adversary the devil walks about like a roaring lion, seeking whom he may devour" (1 Peter 5:8 NKJV). And there you have it, the boldfaced truth—the enemy of our soul is behind it all.

Fortunately, Jesus said, "The Spirit of the Lord is on me, because he has anointed me to proclaim good news to the poor. He has sent me to proclaim freedom for the prisoners and recovery of sight for the blind, to set the oppressed free" (Luke 4:18 NIV).

In fact, the Psalms record, "For He looked down from the height of His sanctuary; From heaven, the Lord viewed the earth, to hear the groaning of the prisoner" (Psalm 102:19–20 NKJV). Therefore, God hears the cry of an inmate, and that day, the prisoner was Sue.

I called, and my name was added to the list for a visit. "Thank you," I said to the operator. "What time can I come tomorrow?"

"Tomorrow? Not tomorrow, lady. There isn't another time slot until Friday."

"Friday!" I exclaimed. "Oh, okay, thank you. Please put my name down, and I'll be there at my appointed time."

Oh no. Sue will be devastated! I thought. I had prearranged for Sue to call the next day.

When the phone rang, I knew it was her. "When can you come?" were Sue's first words.

"Sue, I had to make an appointment, and the earliest time slot isn't until Friday. I'm so sorry, Sue. They won't let me come any earlier!" My poor friend. She was so desperate! Every day, she called and said the same: "Please come."

"I will come soon, Sue. My appointment is Friday."

I awoke Friday morning and prepared myself mentally for the events of the day. It was going to be a bit unusual for me—I was going to jail. My appointment was later in the day, but shortly after lunch, the phone rang, and it was Sue.

"Wendy, they let me out. I was put on a bus and sent back home. I'm in my apartment." *Oh, my goodness gracious,*

I thought. *You have got to be kidding me!* What an emotional roller-coaster this past week had been.

"Okay, Sue. I'm glad you're home. Lock your apartment door, and don't go out, and don't let anyone in! Get some sleep and we'll talk again tomorrow."

All week, I had wrapped my head around visiting her in jail, and now I didn't need to go. I called the jail and cancelled my visit.

Prison Walls

Going to prison had scared Sue to death. "I will never go back there," she said, and she never did.

I've come to the conclusion there are prisons with literal gates and bars, and then there are prisons without walls—and in both surrounds, you feel utterly locked up.

Perhaps you are reading this story and you are in a literal prison—the one with walls—or maybe you are leafing through these pages and living in what *feels* like a prison. Whatever your situation, God loves you.

God doesn't call out to the masses as a whole but to the "one" living within the masses. He calls you by your name. Jesus says,

Come to me, all you who are weary and burdened, and I will give you rest. Take my yoke upon you and learn from me, for I am gentle and humble in heart, and you will find rest for your souls. For my yoke is easy and my burden is light. (Matthew 11:28–30 NIV)

At this point, my sent-for-one assignment took a turn for the worse, and Sue began to get ill—very ill.

Chapter 9

The Final Stretch

A Real Home

Sue called with another new address. She was moving again. This time, though, she started living with her long-time friend Don, who I knew and liked. He was better than all the rest and had a farm job, lived in a little house, and cared about her. Finally, Sue had a place to call home, and incidentally, she kept this house spotless. It's amazing how you feel when you really belong somewhere. Sue really enjoyed living in this little house.

Her Dog, Lilly

Sue loved her dog, Lilly. She was a small dog, not tiny enough to be carried in a purse, but a wee little pup. However, Sue's day-by-day health worsened as her liver slowly failed, and regular trips to the hospital became the norm. Every time Sue was in the hospital having fluid drained from her abdomen, the result of a barely functioning liver, she worried about Lilly.

"Lilly misses me, and I miss her too," she would say. And when Sue returned home from a hospital stay, Lilly was all over her like a bug on a rug. Unmistakably, she was attached to this little dog.

However, a dog is a dog, and while out in her yard one day, Lilly saw a break in the fence and nudged her way through and took off. Sue phoned me, heartbroken; Lilly was gone.

"I have to find her, Wendy! I can't live without my dog. I've been around town calling for her, but I can't find her anywhere." Lilly filled a big void in Sue's heart and life.

After a week or two, Sue called me again. "Wendy, I had flyers printed with Lilly's picture on them and put them in as many downtown store windows as they would let me." Then she said with confidence, "I've prayed for God to find Lilly, for God to send her home."

I knew, of course, God could find her dog, as God can do anything; but to locate Lilly and put her on Sue's doorstep—well, that would be a miracle!

Sue regularly checked downtown to make sure her flyers were still visible. She continued to pray, and so did I. However, I did wonder, *How am I going to explain to Sue if God doesn't answer her prayer? If Lilly never comes back home*?

Right around the two-month mark of Lilly missing, a young man was shopping downtown and saw a picture of Lilly in the store window. The caption read: "Lost Dog." Perking his interest, he took a closer look and recognized the dog. It was Lilly! Immediately, he called his mom and told her that the pup who had been wandering behind their house two months ago belonged to someone. The owner was looking for her dog!

Rather than knocking on Sue's door with Lilly, the mother dropped her off at the address on the flyer and drove away. Lilly, sensing she was home, started barking wildly outside Sue's front door. When Sue heard the barking, she knew God had answered her prayer. She opened the door, and there was Lilly.

She called me so excited, "Wendy, God brought Lilly home! God brought her home!" She proceeded to fill me in on the details.

Our faithful Creator cared so much for Sue that He literally answered Sue's prayer by sending that little pup, Lilly, to her doorstep. Sue was so happy and knew beyond a shadow of a doubt that God had found Lilly and had sent her home.

Now I Lay Me Down to Sleep

Not long after the Lilly miracle, while visiting with Sue, and without any prior thought, out of my mouth tumbled these words: "Sue, starting today, at the end of each of our visits, I want us to pray together. Would that be okay with you?"

"Oh, yes Wendy, that'd be nice," she said kindly.

"Do you know the prayer, 'Now I Lay Me Down to Sleep,' the children's prayer?"

"Yes! I've heard it before," Sue replied.

"Great. At the close of each of our visits, we will say that prayer together."

"Okay," Sue said. And then she added, "We'll call it *our prayer*."

"Okay, Sue, that sounds great. It will be *our prayer*."

Saying *our prayer* became our regular routine. Now, every time I saw her and every time I called her, we would close with *our prayer.*

It's a very simple prayer and had been around since the mid-1700s, and no doubt, has been prayed by millions: Now I lay me down to sleep; I pray the Lord my soul to keep. If I should die before I wake, I pray the Lord my soul to take. Amen.

Sue didn't know much about God, or prayer, for that matter, but those simple words she could understand. That prayer, without a doubt, was an answer to my decade-old prayer, *How do I tell Sue about You, Jesus, in a way she would understand?*

Sick, Sick, Sick

In the last couple years of my journey with Sue, her decades of addictions had caught up with her. She had been at death's door more times than I can count. My children would often inquire as to how she was doing.

"Not good," I would tell them. "I don't think she can live through this new bout of illness."

And they would reply, "That's what you always say, Mom," and they were right. That's how many times I thought she was dying.

Every hospital visit was agony for her. She missed her house, Lilly, and Don. I tried to phone her, if possible, once a day when she was in the hospital and visit her once a week. It was an effort, sometimes a gigantic effort, but Don and I were all she had, so I needed to go.

As I drove the hour to her small town over the years, always my conversation in the car went something like this: "Lord Jesus, I'm doing this for You. All for You, Jesus.

When the end comes for Sue, I don't want my efforts to all be in vain and all the years I loved and cared for her to be wasted. Please, Lord Jesus, guide our conversations and help me to lead her to You before she dies."

Dozens of times, I would walk softly into her hospital room, with the bleached white sheets up to her neck, and wonder, *Is she still breathing? Did she die since the last time the nurses checked on her?*

Oftentimes, she was too sick to talk, so I would just sing quietly. *How much more can one little body take?* I wondered.

Amazingly, the old proverb about a cat with nine lives was certainly true when thinking about Sue. It's a myth, of course—cats don't have nine lives. However, this fable speaks of a cat's ability to survive in situations where they should have been severely injured or dead. And yes, that concept applied to Sue. She was like a cat with nine lives, staring death right in the face and then squirming out again.

I called her once during one of these hospital stays and told her Jesus was with her and she wasn't alone in her hospital room. She peacefully replied, "Oh, Wendy, I know He's here. I feel His squeeze."

I smiled to myself. She was getting it. Not only was she thinking about God, but she was feeling His presence as well. I often think of her words, "I feel His squeeze." What a lovely way to articulate, "Immanuel, God with us."

In spite of Sue's ill health, at times, she would say humorous things. One time, I came to the hospital and she was sitting up in bed and surprisingly, looked reasonably well. I thought to myself, *Wow, what an improvement from last week.* I asked her how she was doing.

"Oh Wendy," she said, "I'm a hundred and ten!"

I laughed out loud. "One hundred and ten percent, Sue! Wow. That's pretty impressive." Here she was, barely alive, and she told me she was 110 percent! I still smile when I think of this, and often, I reply to my husband when he randomly asks, "How are you doing?" with, "Well, David, let me tell you, I'm a hundred and ten percent!"

Another time, Sue was in the hospital and I popped in. "Hi, my sweetheart," I said happily. "How are you doing today?"

"Oh, Wendy, I'm perfect—just like you," Sue replied.

"Sue." I smiled. "Oh, Sue," I said, shaking my head, "I'm not perfect in any way."

"Oh, yes! Oh yes, you are, Wendy," she said adamantly. "You're perfect."

There was no use correcting her. When Sue's mind was made up, that was it. To her, I was Jesus with skin on, and that's what she was seeing: Jesus. *Yes, Sue—you are thinking I'm the good one, but that's not so. I'm a forgiven sinner, it's Jesus you see in me—and you are right. He is perfect.*

How Can She Ever Recover?

Sue would return home for a while and then crash again, her liver failing miserably. One evening Don called to say, "She's in an ambulance on her way to the hospital." She hadn't been doing well for several days, and when he returned from work, he found her on her bed, unresponsive.

The next day, my husband and I went straight to the hospital after work. Once Sue lived in the little house, we often went together to see them both. Sue and Don loved having us drop by. Sue especially loved to see my husband. To her, he was the big, protective, caring brother that she had only dreamed of. When we would come in the door for a visit, Sue would reach up her small arms, and David would bend down with his big arms and gently embrace this little lady. She loved him and always spoke of him in the kindest of ways. David made her feel loved and safe, a feeling that she craved all her life.

We arrived at the hospital at around six o'clock in the evening and found her room number. I went in first, with my husband close behind me. Don was sitting by the window, and after spending the whole day in the hospital, he looked completely spent. We walked softly into Sue's room, and when Don heard our footsteps, he quickly rose to his feet.

"Oh, it's so nice to see you guys," he said warmly with a sigh of relief. Finally, he felt a bit of support.

"She's not good," he said and proceeded to fill us in on the details.

My husband listened to Don's report of the day and glanced over at Sue. Instantly, he knew he had made a mistake. The color began to drain from his face.

David's not a big fan of hospitals and just hates the smell—you know, that sterile, antiseptic aroma. He doesn't like the commotion of doctors scampering about and patients moaning. Then, there's all the noise of clanging trays and medical stuff. No, hospitals are just not for him.

I looked over at Sue, and she was covered in wires and tubes, and not only had one IV but another line where she was receiving blood. The machines were beeping and bleeping, and I quickly looked back at my husband.

"You're not looking too good, David. Maybe you should sit down."

I motioned for him to take a seat on the low-back, uncomfortable, steel hospital chairs—the chairs that seem to beg, "don't sit here long or you will go numb!" David sat down and took off his coat. I thought to myself, *I hope he doesn't faint!*

David has a habit of fainting around sick people. Even hearing about someone who is ill makes him lightheaded, let alone seeing someone who was as sick as Sue. When our daughter April was about seven years old, she cut her finger quite deep and needed several stitches. We lived about ten minutes from town, and David drove her quickly to our local hospital to get looked at.

A couple hours later, I received a call from the nurse. "Mrs. Shelley, we have your daughter here, and she is doing fine. We have her all stitched up and sitting on a chair, actually, beside her dad, who is lying on a stretcher. He couldn't take it watching her get stitched, and the next thing we knew, he was on the floor. He had fainted. I'll need you to come and pick them both up!"

So that's why I said to myself, *David, please don't faint here!* Thankfully, he stayed upright.

I slipped over beside Sue. I'd seen her sick before, but this was the worst. I leaned over the bed and stroked her hair softly.

"Sue," I whispered by her ear. "It's Wendy, I love you." She didn't move a muscle.

Oh my, she looks dreadful, I said to myself. Her face was a stark gray color. *My goodness,* I thought. *She looks like she's dying. No, she looks like she's gone already, but she can't be gone. The machines are still beeping.*

Her eyes started to flutter and then opened wide. Sue stared right at me with big drug-induced, glassy eyes. *It looks as if she is looking right through me,* I thought.

"Wendy," she said slowly, "I love y-o-uuu." Her voice rose as she held the word *you*. Yes, she knew it was me, and over and over she repeated, "I love y-o-uuu" in her raspy smoker's voice. I repeated the same back to her. My sweet Sue. I wondered, *Is this the end?*

Sue was on such strong medication that she slipped in and out of wakefulness. *I can't imagine how she will ever recover from this,* I thought. *She's so frail. This has to be the end.*

After an hour or so, both David and I were tired after a full day of work, so I whispered, "Sue, I'm going now, my sweetheart."

She opened her eyes, but again, they appeared to be blank. However, I didn't want to leave without saying *our prayer*. It was our custom.

"Sue, my darling—I have to go now, my sweetheart, but before I do, can we say *our prayer* together? Don't worry if you can't get the words out. I'll say the words really slow."

Sue immediately closed her eyes, and with me, mouthed the words, every single word, very slowly: *Now I lay me down to sleep; I pray the Lord my soul to keep. If I should die before I wake, I pray the Lord my soul to take. Amen.* Her eyes stayed shut, and she laid still.

My eyes filled with tears. I stayed by her bed sniffling, because I just didn't know. *Will I ever see her alive again? Will she just slip away in the night? Oh, Lord Jesus, I pray the Lord her soul to take.*

I whispered and squeezed her hand, "I love you, my darling Sue. I love you. Goodbye, Sue.

I stepped back from Sue's bed, and with tears pouring down my face, we left her there and walked back to our car. I never expected to see her alive again.

Sue Rallies

Shockingly, she didn't die that night. After spending several weeks in the hospital, she was released to go home, but not without the added care of nurses, who came twice a day. After a week or two, I went to see her at home, and she was sitting up on her little bed, dressed. I could hardly believe my eyes.

"Sue, I didn't think you would live after that last hospital episode—and now look at you!"

She replied, as she shook her head, "Wendy, I have to tell you that was the closest I've ever been to dying. I didn't know I was in the hospital. I didn't know where I was. At one point, I could see myself above my body, and then I heard you call my name. I thought to myself, *That's Wendy's voice*. When I opened my eyes and looked around, I asked Don, 'Where's Wendy?' He told me you and David had come but had left already." Sue reflected for a moment and said to me, "Maybe I was really dying and when I heard your voice, I came back."

Sue was very somber as we chatted; death had never stared her down like this before. With big, loving eyes, she looked up and said, "I don't know what I'd do without you, Wendy. You are my best friend. If you hadn't been in my life, I'd be dead a long time ago."

"Sue, God didn't want you to die without knowing Him. He wants you in heaven and kept His eye on you all your life, and when the time was right, our paths crossed. Remember I told you, it's not enough just to be good, but we must ask Jesus to forgive our sins and make us clean on the inside, so we can go to that better place you talk about. Jesus loves you, Sue, and He sent me to tell you all about Him."

I asked her, "Sue, have you asked Jesus to forgive you for all your mistakes?"

And she replied, "Oh yes, Wendy, yes, I sure have."

I just had to ask; I needed to know for sure.

My sent-for-one journey was in the final stretch.

Chapter 10

The End Is Near

Death Is Coming

It had become quite clear: Sue's time on earth was almost done. Without the help of a cane, Sue couldn't even walk across the floor, and most days, she needed the extra support of a walker to go from room to room. Sue's world was becoming small: she was either in a hospital room in a hospital bed or in her small living room, lying on her little bed in the corner.

When we were together, despite what appeared inevitable, I tried to remain positive. "Isn't it wonderful, Sue," I said one day, "that because we know Jesus, we are both going to heaven when we die?" I wanted it to sound like a twosome, because I didn't want to infer that I thought she was dying. So with a smile I added, "And we'll be together for all of eternity!"

"Oh, Wendy, look at me," she said, shaking her head. "At the rate I'm going, I'll be in heaven before you!" Her answer made me smile. *Yes, Sue,* I thought with a chuckle, *unless I'm in a catastrophic accident, I believe you will beat me to heaven!*

During another hospital visit, routine as they were becoming, Sue told me the priest had come to pray with her.

"Oh, that's lovely, Sue! It's nice to have a minister come and pray for you."

"No, it's not!" Sue replied adamantly. "I don't want him to pray for me. I don't need his prayers—and I even told him so!" My eyes popped open in surprise.

She continued, "I told him: David and Wendy come and pray for me, and that's enough. I don't need your prayers!"

Oh my! I thought. I couldn't help but wonder, *What on earth did the priest think of her outburst?* I'm quite glad our paths never crossed to find out the answer!

Flash forward, and spring had sprung. I was questioning how much longer Sue had to live. The medical staff were trying their best to keep her alive, but it was clear that her liver was shutting down. The nurses and doctors told her, "Your liver is failing. I'm sorry." The pokes and prods that were the hallmarks of Sue's hospital routine were becoming too much for her body to handle.

For the first time in our seventeen years of being friends, Sue uttered these words, pointedly: "Wendy, I'm dying, and I want to die at home." The reality of her life ending was staring her down, and Sue knew there was no way out; her physical body had deteriorated beyond repair.

"Wendy," Sue said reflectively as I sat by her bed, "if I had known Jesus sooner, I wouldn't have been a drug addict."

I put my arm around her shoulder and replied, "I know, Sue. I'm sorry you didn't know Him sooner, but you know Jesus now, and that's what matters. God sent me to you, so you would be ready for heaven when you died."

Sue used drugs and alcohol mainly because she didn't know how to dull the pain in her heart. But as all addictions prove in the end, none of that works long term. It was only when Jesus healed her innermost being that Sue was at peace.

My Last Visit at Sue's Place

I was invited to a wedding shower for my niece in Sue's hometown on a Saturday afternoon in November. Since I was going to be in the area, I thought it was a good time to drop by Sue's place after the party. I called ahead to say I was coming.

"I'm not doing well, Wendy," Sue said, and I could hear it in her voice. "I'm cold, and I don't have enough blankets on my bed."

"Okay, my sweetheart," I replied. "I'm planning on coming this Saturday. I'll pop by, late afternoon. I'll bring a warm blanket when I come." I had a soft, pink, quilt-like blanket at home. I'd give her that one.

It was only six weeks until Christmas, and our family's gifts always included a new quilt, flannel sheets, and an electric blanket. In the last couple of years, because Sue was bedridden so frequently, we also bought her new bedding every Christmas. *This pink blanket will tide her over until I bring her new bedding in a couple of weeks,* I said to myself.

I drove up to the house and thought, *One of these times will be my last. How many more months can Sue survive?*

I had given some thought to Sue's passing and often wondered when—and how—it would it happen. *Would it occur unexpectedly? Would Sue simply die in her sleep? Would I just receive a call telling me that she's gone? Would I have warning? Would I be able to say a final good-bye?*

I opened the door and let myself in. When I came around the corner to where Sue's bed was, she was lying so still. *Oh Jesus,* I thought, *she looks so ill.*

I leaned down and gently touched her shoulder. I felt like a mother, tenderly approaching her sick child. I whispered, "Hi, my sweetheart, it's Wendy."

She roused and looked up at me. "Wendy, you're here… you're here. I want to sit up."

"Oh, Sue. You don't have to sit up! I can talk to you lying down."

"No, I want to visit sitting up." I knew better than to argue with her, so I helped her up.

With great effort, Sue swung her legs over the side of the bed, and we sat together. She looked so swollen. Excess fluid was everywhere in her body, and she didn't even look like herself. Her stomach was distended, and her face looked so puffy. I had trouble holding back a waterfall of tears. *Has she ever looked this bad?* I wondered to myself.

We sat and chatted. "Can you get me my purse, Wendy?" Sue asked.

I reached under the table and handed her a rather bulky, off-white, well-used purse. She rummaged around inside and pulled out her bank statements. "Can you read me the balance?"

I read the balance. "Okay, thank you," she replied. With that, I put the papers back in her purse and slipped her purse under the table. *A little strange,* I thought. She didn't offer an explanation as to the reason for her inquiry—and I didn't want to ask.

I hugged her, kissed her forehead, and told her I loved her. She expressed her love to me as well. "I love you, Wendy, and David too, and all your children," she said.

"I know you do, sweetheart, and we love you just as much."

With that, I said, "Sue, we want to bless you again this Christmas. Can you give me your wish list?" She smiled, thought for a moment, and then gave me her requests. I wrote down what she needed and wanted. "We'll do the same as last year: your gifts and lots of food! I'll bring everything a few days before Christmas."

A short while later, I could see she was tired. "You lie back and rest now, Sue. I brought you a beautiful pink quilt to keep you warm. I'll snuggle you in." Sue laid back down, and I tucked her in like a little child.

"Can we say *our prayer* together, Sue, before I leave?"

With her head against the pillow, and the bright pink blanket tucked under her chin, she closed her eyes tightly and slowly prayed. After a word or two, for some reason, I opened my eyes; from deep within, I watched Sue sincerely talking to her Creator. It was pure sweetness to observe.

I kissed her and said a tearful goodbye, and as I drove away, I thought, *Will I get a call soon saying, "Sue's gone"—or will I have one more visit?*

Three days later, I did get a call. Remember the bank statement Sue wanted me to retrieve from her purse?

Somehow, she gathered up enough strength to phone a taxi and go to the bank. I don't know what she was setting out to do—was she going to take out all her cash, or was she just checking to make sure her money was there? I'll never know. But Sue managed to shuffle her walker just inside the bank doors and shortly thereafter, collapsed on the floor. An ambulance was called, and she never went home again.

The Intensive Care Unit

Don and I were cleared to visit her in the ICU at the local hospital. As I pushed the button for the doors to open in this unit, instantly I heard bloodcurdling screams. "I just hate hearing people cry out in pain!" I said out loud to myself as I walked through the double doors.

I checked in with the nurse, and she gave me Sue's room number. I remember walking down the corridor closer to the screams in the distance, hoping they weren't hers. As I walked further, the screams got closer and closer—those cries were coming from her room. It was Sue, after all.

The doctor had just been in to see Sue and was making notes on her chart outside the door when I walked past. Not wanting to disturb him, I quietly walked around him. However, he sensed someone close by and looked up.

"Are you family?" he asked.

"I'm the closest she has to family, yes," I replied.

"She's been very agitated and crying out all morning. We've just given her another dose of morphine. She's very ill," the doctor replied.

"I know she is, doctor. I'll try and calm her down. She knows me very well. Thank you for all you've done. I know you've done your best."

He looked at me, exhausted, even though it was still mid-morning. With tired, bloodshot eyes, the doctor kindly replied, "Thank you." I wondered to myself, *How many other patients has he tried to keep alive in the last twenty-four hours?*

I turned toward the sound of Sue's cries and went into her room—and upon entering, even I was shocked. She was facing the window, and with both hands gripping the side rails of the bed with her legs pulled up in the fetal position, she was yelling, loud and intermittently. Her oxygen mask was dangling from her face as though she had pulled it off, and her hospital gown was completely open at the back. *Oh, my goodness gracious*! I gasped.

Dashing to her bed, I leaned awkwardly over the rail as I pulled one arm out of my coat, and frantically shook the other arm out as fast as I could, flipping my coat over the bed rail.

"Sue, Sue! It's Wendy. Shhh, I'm here," I whispered as I struggled to give her some dignity and adjust her hospital gown.

"Sue, it's okay—I'm here," I reiterated. She looked up at me with wide, drugged eyes. I scooped as much of her as I could up in my arms, kissed her head, and whispered, "It's okay, my sweetheart, I'm here. Don't yell, Sue. Don't yell. God is with us. It's okay, Sue. I love you."

How do I get the rail down? I thought as I awkwardly leaned over it, *I need this rail to come down!* I was muttering to myself as I struggled with one hand to loosen the latch.

Thankfully, within minutes, a nurse appeared to check on Sue and lowered the rail for me.

Sue couldn't have weighed more than eighty-five pounds by this time—and even that might be a stretch. She was literally skin over bones.

Sue interrupted my thoughts. "You're here," Sue said, her words muffled through the mask yet resonating in the most loving voice she could muster. "You're here," she repeated as an affirmation.

"I'm here, my sweetheart. I love you." Her last dose of medicine was starting to kick in, and she was settling down. For the next couple of hours while she rested, I sat by her bed—praying and pondering. I recalled the scripture:

For My thoughts are not your thoughts, Nor are your ways My ways," says the Lord. For as the heavens are higher than the earth, So are My ways higher than your ways, And My thoughts than your thoughts. (Isaiah 55:8–9 NKJV)

I said to myself, *That scripture is so true*: *God's thoughts are nothing like ours, because how is it that I am sitting in a hospital room watching a drug addict die?* In my wildest dreams, I would have never imagined being in such a situation. I have learned, however, that when we surrender our lives to our Creator daily, He writes His love story through us to others—our spouses, our children, our families, our friends, our neighbors, and even more amazingly, to strangers.

A Nurse's Shock

A nurse came into Sue's room to take blood, so I slipped to the corner of the room to give her space for her blood draw kit. Sue was so tired of being poked and prodded; I was hoping she would manage, though. She didn't look too kindly at the nurse when she walked in, so I wasn't sure how this was going to go.

"Your veins aren't good," this seasoned nurse commented, mechanically and abruptly, as she turned Sue's spindly arm over rather quickly. And with her two fingers, the nurse began tapping Sue's skin, looking for a good vein.

"Yeah," said Sue, reaching up to move her mask slightly. And in a slapstick sort of way, as loud as she could in her tough, I-have-to-protect-myself-because-you're-making-me-look-and-feel-bad kind of voice, she replied, "It's because I used to do crack!"

"What?" exclaimed the nurse as she glanced at Sue. "You did crack?" Even I was surprised at Sue's retort. But the nurse? She was shocked.

The nurse stopped tapping Sue's arm and looked up with startled eyes, and quietly replied, "You caught me off guard. I wasn't expecting that kind of answer."

I chuckled to myself in the corner. Life had forced Sue to be quite witty, and even now, in such a state, she took the nurse and me by surprise. I smiled to myself and recalled my long-ago warning from the guy in apartment number two: "Don't mess with Sue!"

Sue's Getting Worse

The next day I returned, and Sue's breathing was more labored than the day before. As the machines hummed, and before I even entered Sue's room, I stood at the door by the blue curtain. Sue lay so still and looked so much worse than yesterday.

With soft steps, I walked to her bedside. Sue didn't stir. I kissed her head and stroked back the oily, bleached-blond hair off her pale face. I said, "Hello, my darling. It's Wendy."

She opened her eyes slightly, and weakly through her mask, she said warmly, "Oh, hi hon." She often called me hon. Perhaps it was endearing to her. Shortly after, she closed her eyes tight.

Sue Is Dying—This I Know for Sure

I sat by Sue's bed and choked back tears; Sue was dying, and this was the end. *Jesus, be with us. Stay close to us in this hospital room,* I prayed. *Show me how to minister to Sue in these final hours. Love her through me,* I urged.

I knew Sue's passing was imminent, and while she could still converse with me, I approached the subject of dying with the utmost care. I mustered up my courage to be bluntly honest. "Sue," I said, "your body is tired, and it's completely worn out. When Jesus comes for you, it's time for you to go with Him." After knowing and loving Sue for so many years, it was painfully hard for me to choke out those words.

I'll never forget Sue's eyes and the way she looked at me. She turned her head toward me like a child, with a look of absolute and complete trust. From somewhere deep within, at long last, Sue finally allowed a barrier to break and a river of tears gushed down her cheeks—and that river kept gushing. With resolve, she wept in reply, "Okay, Wendy, I will go." Sue had faced the truth: no more going home, and no more getting better, as her earthly life was coming to a close.

"My sweetheart," I said, as we cried together, "you'll be safe in heaven with Jesus, forever. Don't be afraid to go when it's time."

Through her tears, she replied, "Wendy, I'm so happy I'll be safe in heaven. No one will ever hurt me there."

Oh, how deeply it saddened me to hear her say those words! That was all Sue wanted in life: to feel loved, cared for, protected, and safe—but it wasn't until eternity when she would finally receive her wish.

Sweetly, I whispered, "Never again will you be afraid. No one will ever hurt you, and you will be safe with Jesus forever."

"Wendy," Sue continued, "when I close my eyes, all I see is your face. You are my best friend. You, David, and your children are my family. You are good people. I love you all."

"It's all because of Jesus, Sue. Jesus makes us good."

After Sue rested a bit, Sue spoke again. "I would never be alive without you, Wendy. I love you. You are my closest friend," and with a big sigh, she continued, "I can't fight this anymore. I'm too tired to fight sickness any longer."

"I know, my love; you've fought long and hard, just like a soldier. When Jesus comes for you, you go with Him. It's time, and then wait for me to come too, all right?" My heart was crushed as I sobbed out those words.

She smiled and with resolve, responded, "Okay, I will go, and I will wait for you to come."

Through my tears, I assured her of my love. Sue would be in the presence of Jesus soon, and my sent-for-one assignment—this winding seventeen-year journey—would be over.

Chapter 11

Just a Glimpse

Sue Sees Jesus

Did I hear Sue correctly? She was looking straight up at the ceiling with bright eyes as she repeated again, "I see Jesus, Wendy." I lifted her oxygen mask to be sure I wasn't hearing things.

"Sue," I said quietly, "did you say you saw Jesus?" I asked in sheer amazement.

"Yes, I see Jesus." Sue proceeded to portray the sight before her eyes. "He has long, dark hair and has on a robe, a white one, and His hands are open to me."

I watched her stare at the ceiling with a smile that stretched clear across her ashen face. Sue knew nothing about the Bible, or Jesus, or anything spiritual whatsoever. She only knew of the things I had told her.

"I see Jesus, Wendy. It's Jesus!" Sue said excitedly again.

With tears trickling down my cheeks, I replied, "Yes, Sue, I believe that is Jesus. Soon, He will come and take you to heaven." Sue stared straight up, and I looked up as well, hoping with all my heart to catch a glimpse of Him too, even just for a millisecond. Disappointedly, I didn't see Jesus. The veil between heaven and earth was growing thin, but only for Sue.

Sue closed her eyes again and laid very still. I sat by her bed as the reality of this exchange sunk in. The Savior of the world, the Lord Jesus Christ, had appeared to Sue. She'd seen Him, which meant He was in this room. I wept quietly and was comforted; Jesus was here.

While I dwelled on these thoughts, Sue's eyes flew open, and she started speaking again. I sprang to my feet and adjusted her mask to hear what she was saying. "Wendy," she said, "now Jesus is holding two papers in His hands—they look like newspapers."

With her eyes fixed heavenward and my brow furrowed, I wondered, *It can't be a newspaper that Sue is seeing. What could it be that Jesus is holding?*

"Look again, Sue. Would it be a book that Jesus is holding?"

"Yes, yes, Wendy, oh yes! It's a book that looks like two newspapers put together—yes, Wendy, it's a book. Jesus is holding a book!"

With her eyes locked above, I continued. "Sue, remember I told you that your name must be written in God's book so Jesus knows you're coming when you die?"

"Yes, you told me that," Sue said, still fixated.

"I believe Jesus is showing you the Book of Life—and Sue, that's where your name must be written. And because it's there, Jesus will come for you and take you to heaven. When you see Him again, just take His hand and go, my sweetheart. You are ready to go with Him."

As I watched her gaze straight through this world and into the next, I could barely contain myself. What a wonderful Savior! How kind of Him to comfort Sue in her final hours. *Oh, Jesus,* I whispered, *You are just so amazing; there are simply no words to describe You. Thank You, Lord, for appearing to my little friend, just to assure her that she's right with You.*

A Heavenly Orchestra

Sue rested again while I pondered the last hour. Suddenly, she bolted awake. "Wendy, do you hear the music?"

"Music?" I questioned.

Is she dying right now, right here in front of me? I wondered. *Is Jesus coming for her while I stand beside her? Will I just be holding her hand as she passes from this life? Is that how this journey will end? Will Jesus appear to both of us—here, right now—and just take one of us?*

My voice cracked as I adjusted her oxygen mask. "No, my darling, I can't hear any music," I said sadly, listening intently for that heavenly chorus. "I can't hear it, Sue. It is just for you."

"Wendy, oh Wendy, you must hear it! Can't you hear that music?" Sue said with her eyes fixed toward heaven. "It's beautiful." She started to mumble words into her oxygen mask, but I just couldn't make out what she was saying.

I lifted her mask gently and said, "Sue, what are you saying? What does it sound like?" She tried to tell me, but I couldn't piece together her garbled words.

So, I asked, "Does it sound like an orchestra, Sue? You know, where a lot of instruments are playing all at once?"

"Yes, yes! That's it, it sounds like that. Can you hear it?"

"No," I said woefully. Oh, how I wish to have heard what she heard, and to have seen what she's seen. But no, I was just an observer, watching the pure mercy of God.

I leaned in close as she smiled big, her eyes still fixated towards heaven. "Sue, my darling—you're hearing the music of heaven. Jesus is preparing for your soon arrival."

Our Sweet Talk

The next life was becoming more real to Sue than this life was. As I stood by her bed, tears were dropping off my chin and onto my sweater. "I'm in the very presence of God," I whispered to myself in awe. "Jesus is with us in this little room."

Sue's two worlds were mingling—earth and heaven—and I was a witness to this miraculous event. My sweet little friend—the most unlikely child of God—was about to be transported through time and space to be with the Lord forever.

Sue settled again and closed her eyes, and my mind replayed these last couple of hours. I could hardly believe what just happened. *Sue saw Jesus. She's heard heaven's music while still living on earth's side. How does dying get any better than that?*

Sue started to speak again, and I gently moved her mask from her face so I could catch her every word. "Wendy, I talk to Him all the time. I feel Him."

"Oh, my darling, Sue, that's so wonderful. Do you feel His squeeze right now?

"Oh, yes I do. Right now, I feel His squeeze."

For her to speak to me like that, in such a weakened state, was truly a miracle in itself. From time to time, Sue would open her eyes and look to her left, just to see if I was still there.

"Sue, I'm still here," I would assure her, and she would rest again.

After another thirty minutes or so, Sue bolted awake, mumbling. She looked my way, so I jumped up and heard her whisper. "Wendy, you were my only real friend in life. David and your children are my friends too. Your grandkids are mine."

"Yes they are, Sue. My family is your family," I assured her.

Then, speaking slowly, she asked me with great effort, "Tell me again the names of your children, each one of them, and then their children. Tell me all about them again."

I named my five adult children: Tennille, April, Gabriel, Vanessa, and Josiah. I talked about each one of them, and their spouses and their children. I told her how we all loved her and cared about her. She was smiling with grandeur. "I love them all. They are my family."

God's Gift—Just to Me

All the years of loving and caring for Sue culminated in that hospital visit that day. My heart was assured, and I knew wholeheartedly that Sue's spirit was about to take its flight into eternity to be with the Lord forever.

"Keep stroking my head," she whispered. "I love it when you do. I feel like someone cares."

"My darling, you know I care! God sent me to you long ago so you would know He cares too. He loves you even more than I do."

"I know, Wendy. I know," she said softly. I was choked up. Sue's life was draining away right before my eyes. I looked at the clock, and the time had flown by; it was almost time for me to leave again. I stirred Sue gently. "It's time for me to go now, Sue."

Sue blinked her eyes, and with my voice trembling, I asked quietly, "Sue, before I go, can we say *our prayer* together?"

"Okay," she whispered. Together, we prayed slowly, Sue through her mask and me through my tears: "Now I lay me down to sleep; I pray the Lord, my soul to keep. If I should die, before I wake, I pray the Lord, my soul to take." That was the last time we would repeat *our prayer* together, this side of heaven.

When we finished praying, Sue's big eyes looked up at me, and I could feel liquid love pouring from them. "Goodbye, Wendy. I love you," she whispered, and immediately her eyes closed shut. They closed so fast that I thought, *Did she just pass away?* Instantly, I glanced at the monitor. *Is she gone? Did she just die?*

"No," I whispered out loud. "She can't be gone yet. The line on the screen isn't flat."

I stroked her head. "Goodbye, my darling. I'll see you in the morning." Sue was completely still and motionless.

I stood by the door and watched her work for every breath. I felt as if I was struggling to breathe myself. My heart was breaking in two. *How do I say goodbye to her? This little lady I have grown to love so much, how do I just walk away and leave her here?* I couldn't leave. I tried to, but my feet wouldn't walk out the door. I sobbed by the blue curtain and just watched her. Finally, I had to go. I said out loud, "Sue, I love you. Soon, my darling, you'll see Jesus. You've taught me so much about life on the flipside, and loving, and dying. Oh, my sweetheart, you are so precious to me. Goodbye, my darling little friend. Goodbye, I'll miss you."

And with that, my feet trudged down the hall of the ICU, out of the hospital, and back to my car. I drove the hour home.

Sue's Still Alive

That night, I expected a phone call notifying me that Sue was gone, and when I didn't receive a call by morning, I was shocked again. Sue had lived through another night.

I returned to the hospital that evening. Sue had just been given something for pain, so she was resting quietly. With the stark white sheets against her pale graying face, she looked so desperately ill. I slipped over to the side of her bed and kept one eye on the monitor. *When will she stop breathing and go to her better place?* I thought. *Maybe even tonight while I'm here? She's ready; that I know. I'm absolutely sure.*

"Sue, it's Wendy. I love you." Sue moaned a little and opened her eyes slightly. She looked straight at me but couldn't speak. I was shocked by how much she had deteriorated in twenty-four hours; clearly, Sue was near death. I began repeating the twenty-third Psalm, and as her spirit received God's timeless truth, she moaned. Then I began to sing softly "Jesus Loves Me," and I heard her sigh.

I stayed for hours, adjusting her blankets, stroking her forehead, singing, humming, and praying. Before I left, I said to her, "Sue, my darling, I'm going to say *our prayer* now." I prayed slowly in her ear, hoping she might be able to say a word, but she couldn't join me. I heard a quiet rumble in her raw throat, but no words were able to form.

I kissed her forehead, "Goodnight, my darling. I'll see you in heaven. Wait for me there, okay? I love you. Goodnight, my sweet friend."

I left Sue's room and went down the hospital corridor. I walked out of the hospital, opened the door to my car, and sat inside. There, I buried my head in my hands, somewhat like I had done when I met her seventeen years earlier, and cried deep sobs. *Lord Jesus,* I said, *I did all I could for Sue, all You asked me to do.* It was then in this hushed stillness that I heard a gentle whisper deep within my soul. Jesus spoke to me: "I know. Well done."

Still on Earth's Side

To my amazement, Sue didn't die that night either. However, each day I came to visit, she was noticeably worse than the day before, if that was even possible. Clearly, she was at death's door.

At one of my last visits, I stroked Sue's forehead and pushed her hair softly off her tiny face as she slept. All the swelling in her body was gone now; she was skin over bones, with nothing more.

"It's okay, Sue," I said to her. "You will be with Jesus soon. Don't be afraid." From time to time, Sue would open her eyes and smile slightly, but she was too sick to move.

I sang softly by her bed. "Jesus loves me, this I know, for the Bible tells me so. Little ones to Him belong. They are weak, but He is strong. Yes, Jesus loves me. Yes, Jesus loves me. Yes, Jesus loves me, the Bible tells me so." What a beautiful, comforting children's chorus. In its simplicity, the gospel of Jesus Christ is written in those few stanzas.

Two Words

Occasionally, Sue would open her eyes. So I stayed close, rubbing her leg gently and touching her arm or holding her hand—anything to express my love and care in a tangible way. Unexpectedly, I heard garbled words under Sue's mask. I bent down with my ear to her mouth, but her words were too faint to comprehend. She was trying to say something, but I couldn't catch what she was saying. I strained to hear, to listen.

I listened again. "I'm thirsty," Sue said. "I'm thirsty!"

I prayed. *Oh, Jesus! You cried the same words when You, too, were hovering near death. Jesus, my Savior, draw near to us here. Help me, sweet Jesus. My friend is almost gone.*

Sue could no longer swallow water, but I couldn't ignore her request. I dipped my fingers into the cup of water on her nightstand, lifted her mask, and let the droplets fall from my fingers onto her tongue. She licked the water off my fingers like a thirsty baby bird. Her tongue felt so awful, like a piece of worn leather. I kept dipping my fingers in water and dropping the moisture onto her tongue, all the while gently rubbing water droplets into the crevices of her cracked lips, trying to relieve the discomfort of it all. The whole scene before me was pitiful.

"More water," Sue said through her dry, parched throat, as those few drops were doing little to quench her thirst. *Oh, Sue, you're dying,* I said to myself. *You're dying.* I can still picture her stretching her neck and lifting her mouth to me, helpless, trying to catch a droplet of water from a friend who was once a stranger.

I kept up this routine until she finally rested. It was time for me to leave again. I kissed her head softly while she slept and lingered by the door near the blue curtain. The bitterness of sin would soon claim Sue's body, but the sweetness of heaven was just around the corner.

"Sue," I whispered, "my life has been so much richer because I met you. I love you, my friend. Goodnight."

My sent-for-one assignment was almost finished.

Chapter 12

Sue's Gone

Heaven Is Calling

Don phoned the next day. "Wendy, Sue's crashing. The hospital just called and asked me to come."

"Okay, Don, I'll leave right now. I'll be there shortly," I responded.

I grabbed my purse, found my keys, laced my shoes, and was gone. As I drove toward her town, I thought to myself, *This is the end.*

When I arrived at the ICU and walked inside Sue's room, I took one look at her and knew she didn't have long. Sue was so much worse than the day before, and I didn't know how that was even possible. Her long-time friend, Don, was standing by her bed, heartbroken. I had never talked to him about Sue dying before, but we both knew that Sue would never recover; her resilience was spent. Over the last few years, I grew to love Don. He had been a good support to Sue—and besides me, he was all she had.

With tears in his eyes, Don kept rubbing her tiny legs—the little spindles which once supported her body—and I could see he needed comfort.

While wiping back tears, Don said quietly, "Wendy, she's dying."

"I know," I whispered, in tears myself. "She is dying this time."

Over the years, we had both stood in her hospital rooms and Sue always made it back home. But as Don put it, "She's not going to wiggle out this time."

An Unbelievable Question

I could see Don was restless, and I fully understood why. It was painful to be here. *Now that I've arrived, maybe he wants to go*? I thought. Clearly, this whole ordeal was hard on him. Don was shifting his feet from side to side and gestured for me to walk to the end of the bed, out of earshot of Sue.

"Yes?" I queried softly, "Don, are you okay? You don't look very good."

He coughed, and with that deep smoker's rattle and tear-filled eyes, he said quietly, "Wendy, I'm not burying her."

Not burying her? I thought. *What does he mean, not burying her? Don't you bury people who have died? What's he saying, not burying her?*

"Okay," I said slowly, all the while thinking to myself, *What on earth is he talking about*?

In the last few days, I had been thinking about Sue's death, and completely assumed—since Sue only had Don and I—that we would go to her grave together and bury her. I had prepared myself for that ending. *What is he thinking now, and what's he going to do?* I was drawing a complete blank. I waited for him to finish.

"I'm going to have her cremated, Wendy."

Relieved, I thought, *Ah, that's what he's talking about. Cremation. Okay, I get it now.* To be perfectly frank, cremation had always seemed a little creepy to me, so to even consider that option wouldn't have entered my mind.

"Okay," I said, fully complying. "Whatever you think is best, Don."

While Sue continued to breathe rhythmically, with the steady blip of the heart monitor in our ears, Don's next words were uttered: "I can't take Sue's ashes back to my house. I couldn't stand to have her in an urn on the fireplace or something like that. It would be too upsetting." With his head bowed and eyes lowered, he said softly, "I just couldn't do that."

Okay, he's having her cremated and he can't keep her ashes, and he's not burying her. Okay, I thought to myself, as confused as ever. I was trying to figure out where Don was going with this conversation.

Don lifted his head and stared at me, so I just stared back, not knowing what he was trying to say. *Am I supposed to be saying something right now?* I asked myself. The interaction between us was baffling.

Our eyes continued to lock, and an outrageous thought flashed through my mind: *Is he trying to ask me to take her ashes but just can't get the words out? Is that the reason for this awkward pause? No, Wendy,* I scolded myself. *Don't be ridiculous. That thought is absurd! You know nothing about cremation and then being responsible for someone's earthly remains? Wendy, no!*

However, even I was surprised when I opened my mouth. "Don, do you want me to take Sue's ashes?" I asked tenderly.

"Oh yes, Wendy, I want you to take them with you!" His words tumbled out in rapid succession. "Is that okay? Would you do that? I was hoping you would."

Without a moment's hesitation, I said kindly, "Yes, Don, I will. I will take them with me when it's time."

He smiled, relieved, and thanked me.

I could see that Don was done emotionally. "Don, I'm here now. Why don't you go home and get some rest?"

"Thank you, I will." And with that, Don put on his coat, said a tearful goodbye to Sue, and left.

While I sat by Sue's bed, my mind began to spin—not a slow swirl, but an absolutely, out-of-control kind of whirlwind. *What did Don just say? He is having her cremated? Okay, I got that. And what did I agree to? To take Sue's ashes home with me? Is that what I said I would do? This can't be happening.* I shook my head.

Nonetheless, in that moment, I had to lay aside my conversation with Don and draw close to my little friend's fading body. If Sue happened to open her eyes, I wanted to be all in.

However, Sue didn't open her eyes or even stir one iota. She lay perfectly still, motionless, with the white covers folded neatly under her chin and an oxygen mask covering her mouth. I sat quietly and sang softly, watching her chest rise and fall. Clearly, the end was near.

Sue's Last Ten Words

I had been with Sue since midafternoon, and it was now time for me to leave. I stood up and leaned over her tiny body, getting ready to say goodbye, when her eyes flew open. She looked right at me with wide eyes and muttered something into her mask.

Does she even know it's me? I wondered. Since I had arrived hours ago, she hadn't stirred once, so I was shocked that she was awake and trying to speak. *What on earth is she trying to say?* I lifted her mask slightly, trying to understand her mutter, and as I strained and listened again, that's when my heart melted.

Here are the last words she said to me, and in all likelihood, the last words she ever spoke on this side of eternity. Slowly, looking me straight in the eyes and pronouncing every syllable as clearly as she could, tenderly, she whispered, "Wendy, I love you … I love you … I love you."

With tears flowing down my cheeks, I returned Sue's love and told her how much she meant to me. I told her how much I loved her and how God loved her even more. I took her precious little face in my hands, just like a caring mother would do, and said, "I love you too, Sue, and I believe Jesus is coming for you very soon. When He comes, my darling friend, you're good to go."

Sue's eyes closed, and she settled back on her pillow. I leaned down and whispered *our prayer*, but she couldn't mutter a word, open her eyes, or move a muscle. I kissed her with tears cascading down my face and slowly backed up toward the door by the blue curtain again and committed her soul to Jesus. As ridiculous as this seems, I stood there waving and whispered, "Sue, I'll see you in the morning, my darling little friend. I'll see you in heaven. Goodnight, my love." I somberly walked to my car.

I started my trek home and recalled those last precious moments with Sue, and then I remembered my conversation with Don and took a deep breath. *Oh, my goodness gracious. Right. Cremation. Take Sue's ashes home with me. Is that what he asked me to do? Me, take Sue's earthly remains? Did I hear him correctly? Oh my, what am I going to do now?*

What on Earth?

My dear husband—I wondered what he would think of this new development. He had been so supportive throughout this seventeen-year assignment—just so amazingly good. There were so many times when I was in over my head, and David would come to my rescue. He was always understanding, but really, this announcement would shock him. *This will be an interesting conversation,* I said to myself.

When I got home, David wondered how my visit had gone. He knew Sue's death was imminent, and he hoped that I was managing okay. She had been in my life—our lives—for a long time, and David knew I cared deeply for this little lady. I cleared my throat and sat down. He could see in my eyes that something had happened.

"Is she gone, Wendy? Did she die while you were there?"

"No," I said. "She's not gone yet."

Sensing something was up, he proceeded. "Then, what is it? What's happened?"

I started to relay the conversation I had with Don and sheepishly admitted, "I agreed to take Sue's ashes."

David looked at me with wide eyes. "You what!" he exclaimed. "You agreed to take Sue's ashes?" David comes from a big family with lots of brothers and sisters, so a quick response comes ever so naturally to him. His next question to me was, "Okay, Wendy, so where are you taking them?"

"That's just it, David, I don't know." I began rapid-fire thinking aloud. "I was thinking about it on the ride home, and I simply have no idea. I couldn't say no to Don, David. I just couldn't say no to him! That's what Don wanted, and in all honesty, if I could have asked Sue, that's what she would have wanted as well. The only thing I know about cremation is people scatter their loved one's ashes, but there's no way I could do that with Sue. I just couldn't do that. Oh, David, what are we going to do now?" I needed his rescuing again.

Without missing a beat, my husband came up with an idea. "Maybe we could sneak into the small country graveyard down the road—you know, the one beside that old church, just before that little town? We could go after dark and bury her ashes there?"

"David, no! We can't do that!" I exclaimed. "What if we get caught? I don't think you're allowed to sneak into any graveyard after dark with flashlights and shovels and bury people's ashes! David, we can't do that!"

The End

Sometime in the night, they moved Sue to palliative care. The following morning, early, we made our way to Sue's town, and David dropped me off at the hospital's front doors. He had a couple of errands to run that day and would catch up with me later.

I inquired as to where they had moved Sue and quietly walked into her room on the fourth floor. I must say, the room looked gloomy. The walls were a dirty beige color with a single, small, green chair sitting beside the cold, steel hospital bed and a gray side table to the right of the chair. There was no more hum of machines, and there were no nurses buzzing about. There were no flowers, and there were no cards. Other than my family and Don, no one cared about Sue.

Sue was in a blue hospital gown, with a small oxygen mask over her mouth, lying so still. I walked to the right side of her bed, as I had done countless times in the last dozen or so years. But this time was different; this was the absolute end.

I stroked her forehead gently and whispered, "Sue, I'm here, my sweetheart. I'm here." Her eyes were tightly closed as her body shut down. She looked a ghastly gray—I'm assuming the color of death.

"Sue, my darling, I love you," I assured her. But there was no movement, no acknowledgment that she could hear me. I could see death was near as Sue hovered between this life and the next.

"Sue, I love you!" I blurted out. Suddenly, I wondered, *Am I just imagining things or did I see the inside of her eyes move? Flicker just a bit?* I said it again with a little more conviction, "I'm here, Sue. It's Wendy. I love you, Sue! I'm here." Yes, her eyes were flickering beneath the lids! I was sure of it! "Oh, Sue," I said out loud, excitedly amid the aura of death. "You hear me, I know you do! Sue, I'm here. I'm here!" My tears dropped onto the sheets, and I just let them tumble.

An old hymn came to my mind, written by Franny Crosby, the blind hymn writer born in the 1800s, and it fit perfectly. I started to sing softly, as I lingered by her side:

> Rescue the perishing, care for the dying, snatch them in pity from sin and the grave; Weep o'er the erring one, lift up the fallen, tell them of Jesus, the mighty to save. Rescue the perishing, care for the dying, Jesus is merciful, Jesus will save.

I sang, hummed, and watched her tenderly for quite some time; then I heard David's footsteps as he gingerly walked into her room. This space now took on a somber quietness, almost a sacred silence, as we both sensed that heaven was near. Softly, David walked to the other side of her bed, and I sat close to Sue on the right side. We didn't have to figure out what to do next; we knew.

Sue didn't have a minister, nor would she have a funeral. So we gently laid our hands on her tiny body, and our eyes closed in prayer. My husband thanked God for the privilege of caring for Sue and loving her all these years. He thanked Jesus for His mercy, for saving her, that Sue had made herself ready for eternity, and that soon, she would be with Him in heaven forever. Then David committed the keeping of her soul to the care of her Creator, who loved her and was moments away from escorting her into her eternal home.

I knew what was coming next and wondered how I would ever say *our prayer* for the very last time. My heart was crumbling—not from sadness but from the finality of life on earth's side.

David stood silently beside Sue with his head bowed, while I took her feeble hands in mine and prayed: "Now I lay me, down to sleep; I pray the Lord my soul to keep.

If I should die before I wake, I pray the Lord my soul to take. Amen."

"My sweetheart, I love you so much. Jesus is coming for you now. When you see Him, you take His hand and go. Don't be afraid. I'll see you later, my darling friend. I'll see you later."

A few hours passed, and I received word: Sue was gone. In December of 2015, Jesus came for Sue, and she went to be with Him forever.

However, my sent-for-one assignment wasn't quite finished.

Chapter 13

My Final Gift

Home, with Me

The next day, David and I picked up Don at his house, and we made our way to the funeral home in town. Don asked me to pick out an urn, and we made the necessary arrangements for Sue to be cremated.

"Do you want to see her?" the funeral director asked me.

"Oh, yes. I would," I said, surprised. I didn't even know you could do such a thing.

"Okay. You'll have to wait here while we prepare her," he replied.

"No," I said firmly, "that won't be necessary. I'll see her as she is."

"As you wish."

With that, I followed the funeral director down the back stairs—where most people do not typically go—and into the room where the caskets are displayed. He turned the corner into another adjacent room, and I followed, desperately trying not to absorb the creepiness of it all.

The funeral director stopped, turned, gave a slight smile, and made a gesture with his hands.

And there lay my dear little friend, Sue.

Sue was lying on an icy cold stretcher, still in her blue hospital gown. My hand instantly rose to my mouth to cover my gasp, and tears streamed down my face. The funeral director left me alone, and I stood there in utter silence.

I walked to Sue's side and kissed her forehead. It was cold. I stroked her hair—as I had always done before—and held her hand. I even said her name tenderly, but it wasn't the same; Sue wasn't there. Without question, Sue had discarded her earthly tent and was now in the presence of Jesus. I stood there for a few more minutes, but there was no need to linger any longer. This space was completely empty, and my earthly friend was gone.

A week or so later on her actual birthday, a day I would have been with her anyway—I returned to Sue's hometown and brought her earthly remains home with me. I wondered how I would feel, driving home with the ashes of a person in my vehicle. Would I think it strange, or creepy, to have human remains so close to me? But you know, I felt none of those things. Traveling that final hour home was surprisingly peaceful. In fact, it felt perfect. God gave me just what I needed: the right amount of patience, perseverance, love, and courage, right to the end of my sent-for-one assignment.

Since David and I live in a rural area, we decided to keep Sue's earthly remains ourselves, safe and close to us—exactly what Sue would have wanted. In life, and even in death, I accepted Sue as *my* God-given responsibility.

Did Someone Pray?

My husband often wonders that since this journey was so out-of-the-ordinary, was there someone, even just *one* person in Sue's past who prayed for her? I assured him that I didn't know personally of a single soul who did, but did a grandmother pray for her, or a great-grandfather, or maybe an aunt or a great-uncle, or even a volunteer from her frequent visits to the Salvation Army? Or did Sue herself call out, "Oh, God, help me!" at some point in her life? It's such an intriguing thought. However, I won't know the answer to that question until I get to heaven myself. What it does confirm, though, is this: pray for others in your day-to-day life, and never give up on anyone. "The earnest prayer of a righteous person has great power and produces wonderful results" (James 5:16 NLT).

Looking back now, I see the grace of God all over those seventeen years. It was God who kept me loving Sue until the day she died. It was God prompting me with suggestions like, "Give Sue a call today," "Buy food for Sue this week," or "Sue needs a warm coat this winter, and her boots are worn out." God undoubtedly kept Sue on my mind and provided the adequate funds when I needed them to take care of her needs.

A Burden or a Blessing

My son asked me the other day, "Did you ever feel like it was a burden, Mom? Caring for Sue, I mean. Did it feel like a burden to love her all those years?"

I thought for a moment, and answered truthfully, "I didn't feel like it was a burden, son, but I often felt a sort of pressure." I proceeded to explain, "I didn't feel the weight of caring for her in those early years. I was just helping someone who needed a hand. But as the years grew into a decade and beyond, and I realized how much she depended on me, I knew I couldn't abandon her, regardless of the cost to me. So, no, son, it wasn't a burden, but I did feel an obligation. Sue was my God-given responsibility, and I would see this assignment through to the end."

Everyone's Gone

Sadly, before Sue's passing at fifty-four years of age, all her friends I had met over the years, with the exception of Don, had already died from drugs or alcohol-related illnesses.

I kept in touch with Don after Sue passed, since we had become good friends as well. When David and I went to visit him, although Don was happy to see me, he enjoyed talking with David even more. They chatted about all kinds of things. They both loved farming and talked about planting and harvest and tractors. They talked about jobs, or sometimes, just the weather. David always treated Don like an equal—and to someone who lived on the flipside, that was a big deal.

In August of 2017, I called Don for a chat. He told me he had found a good job, something Don had wanted for a long time. Unfortunately, due to Don's addictions, he had a record; consequently, he was often disqualified from places of employment. Once he finally landed a steady job, he was so pleased, and I was very happy for him. We chatted about Sue and how we both missed her.

Our last words on this earth were, "I love you, Don," and his reply, "I love you back." One month after our conversation, Don, too, slipped away into eternity.

I was so heartbroken to learn of his passing. Don suffered from many of the same vices as Sue, and sadly, his lifestyle caught up with him too. I prayed for Don over the years, and many times, I shared his need for a Savior. Don would smile, and say, "Yes, yes, Wendy." Don knew the way to heaven, and I pray he called out to Jesus before he died.

The End

God loved Sue so much that He sent me—the most unlikely—to love her—the most unlovely—but excitingly, Sue is not unlovely anymore! Today, my little friend, Sue, is beautiful, completely healed, totally whole, and truthfully, just started living when she passed away! Undoubtedly, Sue is now 110 percent, as she once exclaimed!

I eagerly await the day when I can talk to Sue and tell her I wrote her story. I want to assure her, though, that I didn't expose her sins to disgrace her as a person, as we are all sinners in need of a Savior; rather, I shared her story to encourage everyone, everywhere that Jesus loves His most prized creation—people—and will go to great lengths to save only one.

And I can hear Sue say to me, "Oh, Wendy! Expose my sins, you say. What sins? There is no talk of sin here. When Jesus forgave me on earth, my sins were totally and completely gone. Forgiven and forgotten. If you thought by telling my story that another one might say, yes to Jesus and come to this beautiful place, then that is perfectly all right with me. Everything you told me about heaven is true. Come with me, Wendy. I'll show you around. Jesus is right through those pearly gates."

I can only imagine Sue's arrival in heaven, as she walked up to that glistening entrance. I envision the look of surprise on her face as she surveyed such splendor. I can almost hear her say, "Is this really heaven? Can I go in there? Is this place for me? C'mon! For me? It can't be!" And then, for her to be escorted into that heavenly place—oh my, that would have been quite a scene!

Can you believe she's already talked to Noah, and he's explained how he built the ark; and she's had a conversation with Moses who parted the Red Sea, a story she's probably never even heard! Sue's met my family and friends who are there and has probably told them she knows me! And then, she's quietly bowed before Jesus, her personal Lord and Savior, who literally saved her from a hopeless eternity.

It's hard to imagine what Sue looks like now, as I've only ever seen Sue tattered and worn; unmistakably, though, I know Sue has undergone the ultimate heavenly makeover, and I'm looking forward to seeing that transformation!

My final thoughts are for Don. I pray that he, too, made his peace with God before he died. I hope, like the thief on the cross, Don breathed his last breath and whispered, "Remember me."

Now, wouldn't that be something—if both Sue and Don are in heaven watching for me to arrive? And I wonder to myself, *Could that really have happened? In Don's final hours, did he recall the prayer he overheard Sue and I pray hundreds of times? Did he, too, call out to Jesus? Is it possible that this sent-for-one journey was actually a sent-for-two assignment?*

And I remember that very familiar scripture, "For God so loved the world that he gave his one and only Son, that whoever believes in him shall not perish but have eternal life" (John 3:16 NIV).

Oh, how I hope they are both in heaven!
Now wouldn't that be something!
Amen and amen, yes, that would be something, indeed!

In Closing ...

Making Peace with God

Sue had accepted Christ's invitation for eternal life and made her peace with God while she was still alive. I imagine heaven's invitation as being something like a wedding invitation: for your name to appear on the guest list, you must accept or decline their request. Heaven holds the Book of Life, or the guest list, and we must reply to this invitation while we are still living on planet earth. Heaven always knows who is coming.

"Behold, now is the accepted time; behold, now is the day of salvation" (2 Corinthians 6:2 NKJV). It is when God's spirit speaks and draws us that we come to Jesus. Sue called it, "God's squeeze," and I pray you sense the same Holy Spirit drawing you today. God is not willing to let you perish regardless of what you have done or how far you have strayed. Or maybe you are a good person; nonetheless, the Bible says we all have sinned in one way or another: "For everyone has sinned; we all fall short of God's glorious standard" (Romans 3:23 NLT). Mercifully, Jesus made a way for us to be reconciled back to a Holy God. Jesus said, "I am the way, the truth, and the life. No one comes to the Father except through Me" (John 14:6 NKJV).

Acceptance to heaven's invitation requires a response—something like this:

Dear Jesus, I am a sinner and am sorry for the wrong things I have done. I ask you to forgive me and fill my heart with peace. I believe you died and rose again, so I could have eternal life. Please make me new from the inside out, and from this day forward, I will try to represent you well. Thank you for saving me. In your name, I pray. Amen.

It's that simple.

Life Lessons Learned

As I reflect back, living Sue's story for as many years as I did has changed me.

I had no idea how the flipside lived or what it was like to be shunned and disregarded, even cast aside, by society. That, dear reader, was a painful revelation. I've learned to love others and expect nothing in return, freely giving my time, resources, and emotional energy. As Jesus said,

But if you love those who love you, what credit is that to you? For even sinners love those who love them. And if you do good to those who do good to you, what credit is that to you? For even sinners do the same. And if you lend to those from whom you hope to receive back, what credit is that to you? For even sinners lend to sinners to receive as much back. But love your enemies, do good, and lend, hoping for nothing in return; and your reward will be great. (Luke 8:32–35 NKJV)

Of course, Sue was not my enemy, but you get the inference here. Jesus is saying to love others and not look for reciprocation, which puts a dent in the armor of our selfish natures. Loving Sue proved to me that it's always worth the risk to move out of one's comfort zone—even to help one person, for years, or even decades—because one person's soul is worth any sacrifice on our part for the sake of eternity.

I learned to show compassion without judgment, to simply reflect the One I was trying to tell her about: the Lord Jesus. Because except for the grace of God, I could have been Sue myself.

Thank you for reading our story, and in some way, I trust that your heart has been encouraged.

God bless you.

Printed in the United States
By Bookmasters